AMONG THE SEA GYPSIES

*An American's Journey
To Finding Fulfillment
With the Philippine Badjao*

Joseph T. Zanetti

Rochelle Rubio

Acknowledgments

While permanently moving to the Philippines was never my intention, it is apparent this is where God wants me to be at this point in my life. It is for this reason that I give thanks, glory, and praise to Him as He has shown great patience and understanding towards me throughout my life.

I would also like to thank Rochelle Rubio, for without her hard work and dedication this book would have never seen the light of day. I would also like to thank the staff and volunteers at the Babina Monare Badjao Learning Center for their dedication and patience towards the Badjao children and to myself. These people include Lady Realda, Ryzza Alejado, Claire Gonzales, Clarence Mosqueda, Jenecyl Omek, and Ebenezer Purisima Jr.

Of course I would like to thank the many Badjao both young and old who have taught me many life lessons over the past two years. Although they may feel that I am doing a lot for them, they have done far more for me, and for that I will forever be grateful to them.

Thanks also goes out to the many supporters of the learning center who have contributed financially and emotionally. You guys know who you are, but I was afraid to acknowledge each one of you publicly as some of you may want to remain anonymous. It would be impossible to keep the doors open without you.

For Teresa –

        Without her, the paths of myself and the Badjao would have never crossed.

I love you.

Contents

Foreword   *9*

Book One: *First World*   15

Chapter 1   A Rascal from the Start   *17*
Chapter 2   The Police Chase   *23*
Chapter 3   The Ticket to Prison   *27*
Chapter 4   Close Call to Murder   *31*
Chapter 5   The Girls at Sandy Level   *41*
Chapter 6   Travels and Run-Ins   *47*

Book Two: *Third World*   55

Chapter 1   My First Sight of The Philippine Badjao   *57*
Chapter 2   The Encounter that Launched Lunches, Friendships, and Changed My Life Forever   *63*
Chapter 3   The Exodus   *73*
Chapter 4   Typhoon Bopha Devastation   *77*
Chapter 5   The Badjao Village   *85*
Chapter 6   The Learning Center   *95*
Chapter 7   Spear Fishing and Apnea Diving   *99*
Chapter 8   Of Factions and Rivalry   *103*
Chapter 9   The Runaway Badjao   *109*
Chapter 10   Learning from the Unschooled   *113*

Revisiting Book Two, Chapter Two   *117*

Appendix   *123*
Badjao Outreach

Foreword

Everyone has a story to tell. But not all have voices. That's what drove me to write this book --- to serve as a small voice to a marginalized, discriminated against and oppressed tribe in the Philippines – the Badjao.

When I made my first trip to this country back in 2011, my goal was simply to have my teeth fixed at a cost that was around eight folds lower than the rate I would have been billed in the US. It was also my opportunity to take a chance on a personal affair which started online.

But other than coming out of the dental clinic alive and with a winning smile on my face, I had no greater expectations.

Come to think of it: I would get the dental work at the same cost of a smart phone plus get to travel to a tropical country which, according to various travel sites and online articles, promises exciting escapades and adventures and an abundance of delectable local and foreign cuisines (or fusions of them) to satisfy one's gastronomic exploits.

My bucket list in the Philippines grew longer and longer as I gathered more information about the country online. The trip would be a great opportunity for an interesting cultural exchange.

What was there to lose?

So off to Southeast Asia I went, halfway around the world from my comfort zone in Eden, North Carolina.

Destination: Davao City, Philippines – a peaceful city on the island of Mindanao.

Mindanao is the second largest island in the entire Philippine archipelago. I didn't mind the news reports about the presence of insurgency groups on the island. Or the occasional travel advisories issued by countries like the US, Canada, and Australia warning their citizens against traveling to Mindanao due to security threats. Or the reported spate of kidnappings of foreigners on some parts of the island or the country as a whole. They could be sensationalized, for all you know.

From my own standpoint, risk is everywhere, not just on this island. I'd rather set out for an adventure than remain "safe" inside a bubble and regret about it in my rocking chair when I'm old and gray.

What good is breathing but not living? From the looking glass, I saw more boon than bane in traveling to this part of the world.

To give you a little bit of background about Davao City, it is one of the most popular and economically developed cities in the Philippines. Its recent economic growth was primarily contributed by the boost in real estate and service sectors. These sectors offset the backlash in agriculture particularly the banana industry which was adversely saddled by blows of catastrophe including the infestation of the dreaded Panama disease in Cavendish bananas, the political and economic tension between China and the Philippines, and the massive devastation brought about by typhoon Bopha in 2012.

Recently, I have seen a noticeable increase in foreign tourists visiting the city. Perhaps part of it is because the local government has been effective and consistent in maintaining peace and order thereby enhancing investor confidence and boosting tourism. Their vice mayor at the time was known for his fierce stance against crime.

I also heard and got curious about their famed fruit called Durian which, as locals put it, smells like hell but tastes like heaven. This thorny fruit is popular in Southeast Asia particularly in Malaysia, Indonesia, Thailand, Brunei and the Philippines and is commonly known as the King of Fruits. The fruit is so famous in the city, it has become a Davao trademark and a must-try for tourists.

To some people, eating Durian is more like a badge of experience than the pleasure of the taste buds. Not trying it during your stay in the city would be like taking a shower without soap.

It took me a couple of months before I mustered enough courage to taste Durian. Surprisingly its smell wasn't as repelling as I expected but it was overwhelming, it was hard to keep a straight face close to it even when the husk was intact. Its soft pale-yellow flesh looked plum and tasteful but the second I sank my teeth into it, I went out of whack. The taste was beyond description. Just love it or hate it. I admire the people who, more than withstand the fruit's potent stench, actually love the taste of it. They say it's an aphrodisiac but I don't really care. Since my first bite, I never attempted to have any Durian again. But at least one item on my bucket list has been ticked.

Tagged as a melting pot of cultures, Davao is home to a mixture of migrants dominated by Visayans, Muslims, and Chinese as well as 10 major indigenous tribes such as Ata, Matigsalug, Ovu-Manuvo, Klata-Djangan, Tagabawa, Tausog, Maguindanao, Maranao, Kagan, and Sama.

Sama alone is a large tribe consisting of multiple subgroups. Not many people know nor bother to know the distinctions among the Sama sub-tribes such as Sama Dilaut, Sama Deya, Sama Banguingi, Sama Sibutu, Sama Siasi, Sama Tawi-Tawi, among others. Each sub-tribe follows distinct customs and traditions. Some are identified as land-dwelling, some are sea-dwelling or at least living close to shore.

Never did I expect that I was bound to meet and forge lasting friendships with some members of the Sama tribe called Sama Dilaut, known to locals as the Badjao.

That's when my life turned around…and I never saw it coming. I divided this book into two parts – the first part tells about the world I used to revolve in back in the First

World and the second part the one I am now living with my new-found Badjao friends in the Third World.

This is not a history book nor is it an ethnography book.

This is a narrative of my actual experiences with my Badjao friends in the Philippines and how they changed my general viewpoints about life and strengthened my spiritual faith.

This is a book about my journey towards understanding a widely misunderstood group of people in this part of the Philippines. I don't claim to know all about them, I simply love them.

In the end, it was them who gave me more lessons in life than I thought I could teach them.

I taught them ABCs and arithmetic. They taught me resilience, freedom, contentment and happiness.

BOOK ONE
First World

Chapter 1
A Rascal from the Start

I will begin my story with the life I used to live back in the US.

I never liked authority. As a kid, I gave my parents a hard time molding me into what society would call an "ideal" son. Straight A student, seldom misbehaved, a sweet young boy who always made his parents proud. I was the exact opposite. Goody two-shoes wasn't me.

In school, I refused to do both seatwork and homework. Who would fail Physical Education in Junior High anyway? I did. Not that I was dumb. I simply refused to pull my weight in class because I disliked being told what to do. I declined to do required activities like swimming (which I later regret because now I'm a butt of joke whenever I waddle like a hybrid dog and frog just to keep my head above water for a minute).

I would just sit there and watch the whole class do all sorts of activities as if they were there for my amusement. But I wasn't an outcast, no. In fact I was very sociable in school.

To me, school was a big playground, an amusement park.

One time in 3rd grade while the parents had a PTA meeting at the school auditorium, I coaxed my classmates to break into the school cafeteria for some pudding. You know that feeling when you wanted something so bad, you would do anything to get it? Any kid in school would probably attest back then that the cafeteria's pudding was so delightfully addictive and we had to have our ration that day.

Unfortunately, we triggered the alarm and caused panic around the campus. The noise startled us but only for a second. It actually stimulated excitement as we scurried laughing in different directions. In our eyes as kids, it was an awesome, though foiled, adventure. To the adults, it was rogue misconduct. I could never understand how the adult minds worked.

My report cards were decked with notes to my parents telling them how playful and stubborn I was and how they have exhausted all their teaching prowess to get me to love acquiring and absorbing knowledge, not just purely having fun. My teachers' long and extensive experiences as educators, no matter how impressive, were no match to my nonchalance to studying.

My mischief once caused our classes to disperse early when I toyed with an electrical outlet and knocked off the classroom's power. How was I to know it was unwise to insert a paper clip into it anyway unless I gave it a try?

I lost count on how frequent my parents were invited to the principal's office to discuss my rascal behavior. Every school invitation they got was a "What did you do this time?" episode at home.

But one thing was clear: my folks never tolerated my naughtiness and misbehavior. They did their best to discipline me. I've been spanked by my father so hard with his shoe until the heel of it broke. I could hardly walk after that.

During those times, parents were not afraid to straighten out their kids like that. While my father did not spare the rod, my mother never got tired of guiding me with her encouraging words.

But I was a tough nut to crack.

In my youth, I was an alcoholic. I drank and partied like there was no tomorrow.

My self-destructive lifestyle got me in trouble with the law pretty often. Not that I was the type who always started a fight but whenever I got in trouble by defending myself, I got caught red-handed.

To say that I was a trouble maker would be convenient as pieces of circumstantial evidence often pointed towards me. Tough luck. Murphy's Law seemed to manifest the most in my life than anyone else's during my heyday.

Or maybe it was because I liked living on the edge. Sounds cliché but it makes sense to say "You can't fall off a cliff without getting near one." I think I read that line somewhere.

Though I seemed like a walking trouble magnet, I could have chosen to avoid it in some instances. The problem was "turning the other cheek" wasn't in my book.

When provoked, I hit back. Tit for tat.

Like when I was with my girlfriend and best buddy Richard partying in a motel room one night. Three guys, who apparently were attracted to my girlfriend, tried to invite themselves in. They attempted to force an entry as they wanted to get to her. They vigorously banged the door demanding that we let them in.

Hollering from the other side of the door, they spewed profanities that disrespected my girlfriend and enraged me. Allowing them in would be plain idiotic.

I knew if I wouldn't call the police, a fight would ensue. So I called the police. But it wasn't to protect us but them. Modesty aside, I was afraid we would beat those guys to a pulp if they didn't stop provoking us.

The problem was, the door was about to give in. By the time the police would get there, so much would have happened. Not much of a choice there. Either we fought or got mauled. We chose to fight.

When you corner a snake, you don't expect the snake to cower. You expect it to attack.

I put my weight on the door and grabbed the doorknob with my right hand and a glass bottle of orange juice on the left, ready to give them thugs a grand entrance.

Richard took out his belt which was a heavy chain with a padlock as a buckle, it was more of a weapon than a fashion accessory.

Nodding at Richard as a signal to prepare for combat, I swung the door open just enough to let the first guy fit halfway. I smashed the half gallon bottle on the guy's head, it took him out on the first blow. I could almost feel his pain as he twisted in agony on the floor, clasping his head with his both hands.

His left cheek was dripping with blood.

I obviously hit him a bit too hard but hey, he asked for it.

(That wound left the guy with a big scar that he's had to wear up to this day. But the important yet ironic thing was, we became friends over the years.)

One man down.

That left the playing field even, one was to one.

Richard and I dashed out the door and took the fight outside. We didn't want to pay for damages to the motel when the brawl was over. More importantly we had to make sure they couldn't get to my girlfriend.

When the police came, three men were sprawled almost motionless on the ground. Luckily they didn't include me and Richard. We battered the guys to the point that we ended up being the ones arrested by the very authorities I called. How ironic was that?

And we still ended up paying for damages to the motel's door and window.

Chapter 2
The Police Chase

One peaceful night in a parking lot in Reidsville, Richard and I were sitting in my convertible drinking beer, quietly minding our own business, and hoping to hook up with some girls if we got lucky.

It looked like an uneventful night far from the usual chaos we often got caught up with while we were out. Then a cop disrupted our solitude.

"Can I see your driver's license?" the cop asked, looking at me like he was evaluating me in a dark interrogation room with a single light bulb swinging right over my head.

So I put my beer down on the dashboard, reached out for my driver's license, handed it to him, and let him do his noble job. Then he left us alone, secure in our moorings. It sounded too easy. But that's not what happened.

What really happened was Richard and I laughed at the cop's face and did not bother to do as told. Instead, I looked back at the officer with a mocking face and said "I don't think so" before I hit the accelerator and sped off.

That started a long, tenacious police chase that could potentially make a good scene for a Hollywood production.

Upon reaching a nearby intersection, a police car was already waiting on us with its red light on, like a bull ready to attack. This cop was obviously radioed by the cop we ran off from. Battle-tested, situations like these got me more excited than scared.

"And I thought this was going to be a humdrum night," I mused.

Driving at speeds up to 100 miles per hour, I sped through highways, outskirts and off roads to escape from the pursuing cop. The cold wind pierced though my skin like thousands of minuscule ice crystals. It felt good on my warm face flushed both by beer and adrenalin rush.

The noise from my screeching tires and the siren from the police car broke the silence of my tranquil neighborhood.

We had a blast as if we were drag racing with a cop.

Our hyped-up and alcohol-driven laughter ripped through our automobile noises as we painted the town red in own brand of action.

Richard, who was seated beside me, turned around in his seat and reached out for the big cooler full of beer cans at the back seat. He hurled the cans at the tailing police mobile as if the cans were hand grenades. But either Richard was too drunk or I was driving and swerving too good at full speed that not a single beer can hit the police car. In that case, I had reasons to believe it was more like the former.

The chase, which began in Reidsville, did not end until I ran out of gas in Stoneville, NC.

Had I been thinking straight, I would have veered off towards Virginia where the NC police had no jurisdiction and therefore could not chase us down. (But of course since beer occupied the spot where my brain should have been, I wasn't able to outsmart the cop that night.) Or maybe it was more appropriate to say that had I been thinking straight, I would have flashed my driver's license when the cop asked me to. Then all of this hullabaloo would never have taken place.

Richard ended up being slapped with nothing but littering (thanks to his all-missed attempts) while I collected multiple charges that I could hardly memorize.

The incident landed on the news the next morning. Much as I would have appreciated being a news maker one day, I never preferred it to be about me breaking the law. But then again, what was I expecting? Certainly not a story about me being handed a Nobel Peace Prize. That would be expecting an apple tree to bear grapes.

Chapter 3
The Ticket to Prison

I was a deviant. I followed my own rules, my own terms. And Richard was always there to back me up. We were inseparable. A tag team.

Even when I served the US military in my late teens and was assigned in Europe, I took long vacations from my accumulated leave credits so I could go back home to the US and do all crazy stuff with Richard. If there was one word to describe our lives back then, it would be PARTY.
Being both single and earning, money was not an issue. Richard and I splurged on booze like water.

However, Richard always got the beating from my mother who had branded him as the bad apple. Perhaps it was easier for her to believe that than to accept the bitter reality that it was her own son dragging Richard to the wild side and not the other way around. After all, I had a smile of an angel --- that innocent look in the face that could disarm any suspecting soul…unless I was caught in the act (which happened quite a lot anyway).

One night, Richard drove me home from yet another night of boozing. I was too drunk, I had to crawl into my bed and pass out in a second. Unable to contain her patience, my mom berated Richard for the wasted kid I have become and blamed it all on my equally wasted friend.

Their heated argument escalated in violence. Mom grabbed a shock absorber that was lying on the carport, drove her car and chased Richard down to his house. I never would have imagined my sweet mom to go berserk like that. Richard could have pulled a trigger that detonated her.

In retaliation, Richard drove back to my parents' house and threw a Molotov cocktail right into my sister's bedroom. The blast woke the entire neighborhood except the deadbeat me. Not even the earsplitting wails of sirens from the fire truck that responded stirred me back to consciousness.

My parents' house almost went up in smoke yet I didn't even know about it until morning when I finally woke up sober.

It was sheer luck that my sister decided to sleep in another room that night and was spared from what could have been a fatal attack perpetrated by my own beloved friend.

All through the night I was oblivious to all the chaos in and around the house. I could have been grilled alive and not know it if the fire was not contained in time.

What could have been the headlines the next day? "Man Too Wasted, Burned Alive" or "Too Drunk to Save Self, Man Trapped in Burning House." I would have died not from burns but from shame.

Finally, the incident became Richard's ticket to prison.

I felt bad that that incident had to happen.

Richard obviously let alcohol got the better of him. It took control of his behavior yet again, like it always did to me. Another classic example that too much alcohol shrouds one's ability to think rationally and morally. He could have killed my entire family including me, in my own bed.

Our family decided not to press charges against Richard but the state did and locked up my partner-in-crime away for more than a decade.

If I felt terrible for Richard, I wonder what kind of horror he could have felt for himself when he heard the court's decision. More so, I wonder what kind of horrors he faced everyday behind those bars in the many years that he was supposed to be in his prime.

It scared me to see that one false move could actually suck your life away. Richard learned his lesson the hard and long way.

I wish my buddy had the same chance of redemption like I did. Eventually I grew up. Got tired of the lifestyle I used to live. Picked myself up and assumed big responsibilities like having a family of my own, taking care of them and making my small but flourishing marks in the business world.

Chapter 4
Close Call to Murder

It almost took a friend's life, Jerry, for me to finally wake up and change my mindset about life in general. (And you thought I learned from Richard. Told you I was a hard case.)

I was in my early twenties and not long being out of the military.

In one of those house parties I hosted where I've had more liquor than water in my system, my friends and I decided to do some pranks outside. We took to the streets, leaving behind my girlfriend with my friend Jerry and a 14-year old girl still partying at my place.

Our group merrily marched down to a bridge in Leakesville, one of our favorite places to hang out in town. Our favorite thing to do there was scare people.

We would have one of our friends stand up on the railing at the side of the bridge, facing out over the water. Once we saw a car approaching, the friend commissioned to scare would act like he was ready to say goodbye to the cruel world.

He would stretch out his arms in the air and tilt his head up like an act of total surrender. He must do it in full view of the coming motorists or else the act would be in vain. Then just as the coming vehicle was close enough, he would jump off the bridge, which some people didn't know to have a narrow walkway along the side.

The walkway was a few feet lower than the bridge hence, unless you live around that area, you wouldn't know it exists. It was on that low walkway beside the bridge where our acting friend would actually land safely after "taking his own life" and where I and the rest of our friends would be waiting and laughing.

Most of the time, the passing vehicles would pull over and petrified people would peer into what they thought was the "depths" of the river, only to find young people like us making a mockery of their genuine concern. Guilty as charged. We played with people's emotions and time.

We definitely bothered several people with the series of pranks our group notoriously made on that bridge. Some may have found the prank funny while some may have been pissed with our insensitivity. They all had the right to judge us the way they wanted after we disturbed their peace.

Quite frankly at that time, we didn't care what people thought about us. We were all to ourselves and we had the audacity to blame it on our youth. "We're young and free, we can do whatever we want. We won't be young forever." These were some of the most abused mantras we lived by.

Satisfied with our gag attack that night, we walked back to my place sniggering as we recalled the night's highlights.

About one mile away from my house, we saw Jerry's car parked in front of a barn. As we drew nearer, we heard some grunting and moaning coming from the inside. They were unmistakable noises of intimate pleasure.

"I left my girlfriend with Jerry," was all that was pounding in my head like migraine. I smelled rats.

Paranoia suddenly flooded my thoughts and stuck solid in there like a rock. I already believed my own fear as if it had been proven true. I felt my blood boil as I cocked my gun. I wanted to blast open the door at that instant.

Walking towards the barn felt like a hundred miles of toddling in slow motion despite that I was only about 10 steps away from its door. I have never felt so impatient.

"Who's in there? Come out or I'll go drag you out myself!"

I yelled to the top of my lungs like a madman. I had a strong feeling that I knew the people inside and I couldn't wait to exact revenge. All hell would break loose.

Silence fell and everyone could feel the tension.

"Come out now!" I called out again with wrath in my voice.

I staggered to hold my temper.

Slowly, the barn's door creaked open. Just as I suspected, my friend Jerry appeared from the small opening. He looked terrified, looking half a mess with his shirt worn haphazardly. Obviously he had no time to fix himself. He had no idea that I was more horrified to see that my nightmare was becoming real.

I felt my fury devouring me like poison.

"I knew it!" I muttered under my breath as I gripped my gun harder. It was impossible to contain my rage any longer.

"Kneel!" I commanded Jerry as I pointed my gun at the back of his head. He was no more than a traitor to me.

Shaking, Jerry kneeled on the grassy ground without any attempt of resistance. He was smart not to fight back.

"Who's in there?" I shouted as if he was deaf. He was too frightened to even open his mouth and try to talk his way to freedom. He knew that as mad as I was, I could easily pull the trigger if he even made an effort to outwit me for a second.

"Call out whoever's hiding inside or I swear I will shoot you right now!" I threatened. Jerry hesitated. At that point, I concluded that it was my girlfriend he was hooking up with inside. His reluctance gave him away. Calling out my girlfriend for all our friends to see in such an awkward situation would be tantamount to dying.

"I will not hesitate to blast your head off right now and I will not feel any remorse," I declared with conviction. I wasn't kidding.

Our friends tried to intervene but my rage muffled their voices. No amount of diplomatic attempts could cool me down at that moment. It's flabbergasting how jealousy could make a man lose all his balance.

Then the heavy barn door squeaked loudly beside me. I turned to see a set of pretty hands slowly pushing it open. I felt my heart throb. I dreaded to see my girlfriend coming out of the shadows.

A frightened, pretty face emerged from the barn's darkness and into the light outside where we were all huddled in a commotion. We stood there in silence at the sight of her. I was lost for words.

It wasn't my girlfriend. It was the 14-year old girl at the party.

That explained Jerry's reluctance. Though he wasn't guilty of sneaking out with my girlfriend, he was guilty of a more serious and shaming offense. Sleeping with a minor was insanely disgusting. Not only would it lock you up in jail for many years but more importantly it would also mess up the minor's life…forever.

The rage I felt just a few moments ago dissolved into shock and disbelief. While I was relieved to see that it wasn't my girlfriend, I was disturbed that it was a child.

Despite the girl's not-so-immaculate reputation, the fact still remained that she was a minor. Apparently, we learned that Jerry wasn't her first either which led me to believe that she must have had a troubled childhood. One that none of us there standing in front of her could probably handle. At her age, she needed guidance and real love, not a false display of affection masked by carnal gratifications.

A man who would take advantage of a distraught teenager like her did not deserve to fall into the category of humans. Though I despised Jerry for what he did, the revelation snapped me out of my idiocy. Putting the law into my own hands would just be as bad as what Jerry did. So what difference would I make?

That served as my turning point.

I could have landed on the news again the next morning, and this time I could have made it on the front page for killing my own friend in front of our peers as witnesses. How stupid was that? I was too close to blowing Jerry's head and it all stemmed from plain paranoia.

The incident could have haunted our friends for the rest of their lives for failing to stop an impending crime. They could have been forever traumatized by the booming sound of my gun and the graphic images of Jerry's blown-off brain on the ground and probably grossly splattered on their skin.

It's terrifying how one bad spur-of-the-moment act could turn your life upside down and cause a lot of emotional stress not only to yourself but also to the people around you --- the people who love and care about you.

If I pulled the trigger that night, it would have been the start of my hell on earth. And I could have dragged my friends along into my self-inflicted miseries.

That night, I finally said goodbye to the war-freak me.

I focused on making a living and staying out of trouble.

Eventually I put up a club with three of my friends and one of my cousins. It wasn't that easy to do away with being a party animal hence I chose that business. I never had to feel that I was working all night. I was practically partying and getting paid for it. The best of both worlds.

However, like in any other businesses, the club was not an easy bed of roses. We had our first major bump right after the opening night. One of our business partners, a close friend whom I have known since childhood, ran away with the night's revenue worth $7,000. We never heard about him since.

Eventually, we survived the birth pains. We managed to grow the business and became a popular go-to place in town. Our patrons multiplied.

It was where I met my wife who was then working as one of our waitresses.

Over the stretch of a single year, the business had its highs and lows. We reached the point where we staggered to keep the club going due to its demanding schedule. One by one, my friends started quitting and I was left to run the business alone.

Since it was a bar at night and a restaurant during the day, I worked around the clock from 7 am to 4 am every day, 7 days a week. I had power naps instead of full nights' sleep. Work became the center of my world. I barely had time for my family, for myself.

Work consumed me.

When the club folded up, I bought a 18-wheeler cargo truck and spent most of my time on the road. While it brought in a lot of money for the family, it took my time away from home. I drove under all kinds of weather.

Several other ventures came, one after another. I opened a car wash, then a restaurant, sold Italian Ice from a cart, and eventually saved up enough to open an Italian ice shop.

In every new opportunity that knocked on my door, I couldn't wait to get my feet wet.

I worked all the time to provide for my family and seeing my efforts paying off financially pushed me to work even harder.

I was able to build a 2-story house with 4 bedrooms and a spacious basement. The house was filled with not only comfort but also luxury.

One fateful night, I had a call from my father. He, my mom and my sister were inviting me to a family dinner. I couldn't go. I had to work.

The following morning, I got another call from my father telling me that mom was rushed to the hospital and that I needed to go. Still I couldn't go. My hands were full. I had to work.

It took me an hour before I caught up with them at the hospital. At the hallway stood my father, sister, uncles and aunts. They just gathered there waiting for me outside the room where my mom was. They all looked sullen.

It was then that it dawned on me that mom was gone.

It occurred to me that life is as feeble as a candle. Tomorrow holds no certainty that we would still be around.

If I was to lose other members of my family tomorrow, would I really want to be working instead of spending quality time with them while they're alive?

It was a painful experience that shifted my paradigm. Family first. I trimmed down my work time and went home in the afternoon to play with the kids. I had more room for family recreation than ever.

As a relative consequence, our family income was cut in half. Sacrifices had to be made. Our lifestyle had to be adjusted. The kids couldn't go to dance and soccer classes anymore.

Ironically, the family that I loved so dearly and worked so hard for fell apart.

Coming home from work one afternoon, I found the house empty. All the furniture, appliances, my family's clothes, even the light bulbs were gone.

The kids' laughter which used to bounce off the walls in all corners of the house was no more but an echo of the past.

My family has left me. All that remained was the stone-cold house. Lifeless. Meaningless.

I was all by myself.

Chapter 5
The Girls at Sandy Level

While I was married to my ex-wife, I used to drive around in the middle of the night to pick up prostitutes and take them to hotels and abandoned houses. Wait, let me explain, it's not what you think it is.

If you have gone to or at least read about Sandy Level also known as Log Town, a small town located just across the state line in Virginia, you might have known about its dreaded reputation of cuddling drug dealers and all sorts of outlaws --- the kinds who would go on a killing rampage like a recreation. The kinds who mock the laws of the land in the name of crack.

Hardened criminals in that town do not fear the Police. It's the other way around. The town Police, outgunned and outnumbered, wouldn't dare penetrate the area unless they want to commit suicide.

That's where I picked the girls.

I would go into the notorious town to look for girls, not to worsen their predicament but to rescue them. That's where I met Denise.

I found Denise wandering aimlessly along a badly-lit road with a bloody kitchen knife in her right hand, painting the sidewalk with a trail of crimson drops. Her hair was a tousled mesh of brown covering half of her face. Her frilly white dress would have looked pretty on her if it wasn't badly-torn and smudged with what looked like fresh blood.

Under the moonlit sky, she looked like a character out of a suspense-thriller movie.

I slowed down to keep with her pace until I got her attention.

"Do you need a lift?" I asked as I pulled over to the side. The look on her face was a combination of surprise and caution.

She looked shocked by my bravado to offer a ride to a stranger like her who looked like she just killed a man. At the same time she held herself guarded, perhaps thinking that I was a psycho who was intent on making her life a living hell, if it wasn't already.

"Can't you see I have a knife?" she retorted.

"Yeah, I see that," I said matter-of-factly. "I also see that it's not safe for you to go walking around like that and thought I could help you." At the back of my mind, I was strong and skilled enough to restrain her in case she goes gaga and tries to stab me once she's inside the car. Who knows, she could be mental? Or what if some low-lives were trying to hunt her down at that moment? I was putting my life in danger. I should be the one more cautious instead of her.

She hesitated. I urged her again to get in the car. Still, she refused.

"Look, I understand trusting a stranger is not a good idea but what better option do you have, really?" It got her thinking. "I can get you out of here safe and fast." I sounded like a desperate salesman.

Finally, Denise took down her wall and hopped in the car. The smell of blood filled my nostrils. It was nauseating.

"What happened to you?" I asked as I drove off.

Denise started talking freely. She just stabbed a couple of men with the knife she was holding.

She was a victim of drug addiction and sexual abuse. Her drug dependency pushed her down to the pit of moral decay. She needed drugs more than her finances could handle. Ultimately she couldn't afford to buy cocaine and the pushers in Log Town made her pay for it with sex.

Several men held her captive inside a house for days. "They wouldn't let me leave," she recalled sobbing. "I had to defend myself." Her eyes were full of indignation when she said that. The look of a woman violated many times over until her heart could feel no pain, just hatred, loathing. Her conscience calloused.

After I took her out of town that night, I never saw her again.

I tried to save as many women and young girls in Sandy Level as I could. I patrolled the area like a police officer for 8 long years.

I wanted to change lives, one woman at a time.

"You don't recognize me, do you?" said the woman I just picked up to transport out of Log Town. I paid more attention to her face. She was a complete stranger to me.

"No. Have we met before?" I asked. She wept so hard. What did I say? I could see she was terribly sorry for herself. She looked at me with tears in her eyes. "I'm Amy."

"Amy," I echoed. I remember her now. She was one of my sister's good friends --- the girl that I liked back in High School.

I felt a pang on my chest. How did this happen to her? She looked decades older than her age. Nothing about her now resembled the youth and vitality she radiated when I adored her in silence back in school.

We talked about old, happier times. It was that brief moment that I saw her smile again.

I dropped her at an abandoned house in Eden where I was confident she would be safe. We prayed together before I left.

Many people knew about my activities there, even the pushers and other outlaws hiding in Sandy Level. The only reason I was able to roam freely in that dreaded area and execute my personal mission was that I was friends with some of the "big guns" there.

I played in the middle. That was the only way to survive. I felt that it was my moral obligation to liberate victims in my own little way but it wasn't my duty to go after criminals.

I could have turned in some pushers to the Police but I could have been dead long before the Police captured the people I turned in.

I am not Chuck Norris.

I heard that one elderly woman took the courage to tip off the authorities about the drug pushers she knew. It didn't take long for gunmen to find out about her. Her house was peppered with bullets. So was her frail body. I had no plans of taking the same route.

To remain alive, one should observe the code of silence. One of the women I tried to save was Andrea, a childhood friend. We grew up together in Eden. I didn't know how Andrea got into that kind of mess. She was a sweet girl from a decent family. She did well in school.

There was no indication that she would waste her life away with drugs. I took her out of Sandy Level where poor women like her were vulnerable to all kinds of abuses known to man.

But I could only do so much.

A few years later, I found her name on the news. She was found dead in an open field in Virginia, with a shotgun blast in the chest.

Chapter 6
Travels and Run-Ins

By age 21, I have traveled to about 20 countries around the world.

I have explored the majestic architectures in Germany and seen the world-famous Gothic architectural wonder of a monument called Kolner Dom, known to many as Cologne Cathedral. Walking around this humongous landmark with other equally fascinated tourists was like touring a myriad of art shows in the middle ages.

It felt more like a time travel to me where every step I took around the colossal structure seemed to siphon me deeper and deeper into a whole new dimension, taking me back to the renaissance era of marvelous arts. It was a jaw-dropping experience that not so many people could have in their lifetime. I was one lucky guy to have the means and opportunity to be there and touch the walls that were older than my great grandfather but which strength did not wither.

I stood so small to its might and grandeur.

I could almost see the ghosts of the men and women of old who must have devoted half of their lifetimes working on the intricately carved stones, gigantic columns, and baroque ceilings and altars, among others that made up the historical cathedral.

These were all glaring attestations of man's artistic prowess that could withstand the ages. Its enormous beauty survived the devastation of World War II when warring countries used it as a landmark, hence it was never bombed. It was one of the few structures left standing when all the war dust settled.

Every corner, every wall, ceiling and floor, practically every nook and cranny is a brilliant masterpiece. No wonder it took them more than 600 years and countless masters of visual arts to complete it since its foundations were laid in the 13th century (though of course, there must have been more to the delay than that premise).

I have wined and dined and got beaten up black and blue, I almost died.

Here's how it happened (Buckle up, this is a major confession): I have a penchant for saving people. Okay, you may laugh now. But hey, it's not a superhero complex coming from a bloated ego but from an honest-to-goodness urge to help others even strangers.

Fine, I'm no Clark Kent nor Peter Parker nor Tony Stark nor Bruce Wayne but I wouldn't mind being any one of them except that I would rather eat pins than wear tights that would show my beer belly (so I guess that leaves me with the Iron Man suit).

My late mother used to tell my father that I care too much about others and it could potentially do more harm than good, either to me or the subject of my err…concern. In this case, my heroic act (or at least my noble attempt to save a girl I didn't even know) left me half-dead in the lurch.

One night, I was tottering down the streets of Mainz somewhere in Germany with my friend Carlos. We were taking some time off from the US military base we were stationed at and had a little too much beer.

Around a dimly lit bend we heard a muffled cry. Our curiosity led us to a weeping woman, probably in her early 20's, looking perplexed and inconsolable, her nose bleeding and her lip cut from what looked like a glaring evidence of physical violence. The compassion in me took over like an autopilot.

It was that tense moment that called for the popular line "This is the job for…" in the movies and comic books.

Seriously, I wasn't going to take it sitting down. Forget the old adage "Mind our own business." In situations like these, that maxim doesn't sit well with me.

"Excuse us, miss…Can we help you?" I said.

"Some friggin' jerks punched me in the face," the lady said in between sobs.

I could hear my knuckles crack in rage. It was enough to fuel my resolve to find the cowards and make them all pay.

This was no way to treat a woman.

With my fully-charged superpower drive to bring forth justice, Carlos and I left in a huff, resolute to wage war against some thugs and put them in their proper places. It was going to be an action-packed night.

We stormed the pub that the lady pointed right in front of us. We went up to the pool table as we entered the bar, I almost thought we just entered an entirely different country as we met the blank stares of the Turkish-looking men dominating the place. But that didn't distract me from my goal.

"Which one of you hit the girl out front?" I belted out which I realized as quickly as I said it, sounded like a bad script for a B movie. The men went on with their business as if we did not exist. They probably thought Carlos and I were nuts and not worth their display of combat skills. After all, nobody with a normal sense of danger would dare provoke a fight in a foreign country with some 20 men gawking around them and who's fighting skills and personal backgrounds they probably would cringe about.

Blame it on the beer for giving us that feeling of invincibility.

I went on with my tirade. I started nitpicking at random, demanding a response. "Only chickens hit women. Come out of your egg shells!"

Still no response. How embarrassing.

I walked over to a pool table where some 10 serious-looking men were huddled for a game. They looked so deep into it as if the pool table was a shrine. I reached out my hands on the table and dispersed the cue balls.

A perfect recipe for disaster.

In no time, pissed off men started inching forward, towering me. At that moment I didn't know if Carlos was still behind me or has scampered out for safety. Nevertheless, it was easy to see I was outnumbered. And when the first blows of fists and probably feet came flying from all directions and landed on every part of my body, which made it impossible for me to ever diffuse my superhero punches and antics, I knew I was right.

I don't know what happened to Carlos but I woke up half dead on the sidewalk with an old man wearing a gray coat and a gray hat checking my vital signs. What was left of my consciousness was all I could muster to converse with the old folk who was trying to get me to safety (which means salvaging me from the streets and onto a train) in exchange of $2.

The next time I woke up, I was on a train with two police officers. They were combing through my wallet and talking about how hot my girlfriend was in the pictures. I was too beat up and drunk to take offense in all their indecent comments about my girl. Shame how I stood up for a stranger but I could not lift a finger to defend my girl's honor from these scumbags in uniform. The same scumbags I loathed ended up giving me a lift home. Indeed, sobriety (or in my case involuntary sobriety due to alcohol and injury) saves us from troubles.

It wasn't the only time I had a brush with death. In my memorable trip to the German Alps, I braved the icy slopes of Berchtesgaden. No, it wasn't as taxing as it sounds. I only got as far as where the vehicles would drop the tourists for sight-seeing and photo-shoot. At least I could say I got to the foot of the mountain, which to a man who would rather party than hike like me, was a feat.

The trouble happened when I went out to drink one winter night. To get back to my hotel after a heavy alcohol party, I had to waddle in waist-deep snow. I could have died of hypothermia. Should I have passed out that night, they wouldn't have found my body until Spring. Or in some bizarre circumstances where the ice around me wouldn't melt, I would've been preserved in maybe a thousand years and ended up in a science lab as a specimen.

I don't know how I shuffled through safety but I would like to think that perhaps alcohol made my body warmer and more resilient to the cold (even though there have been scientific studies that prove it's a myth and that drinking alcohol actually lowers down your body's core temperature. Ergo, consumption of alcohol in a cold weather easily spells disaster).

In between memory lapses, I recalled helping a stranger push his car out of the snow. Then I walked to my hotel like a zombie where my visiting parents and sister were waiting.

Looking back, I have lived an exciting life. Fulfilling? Not quite. That's a lofty adjective to claim for a life like mine. I have frolicked in the majestic marine treasures in the Bahamas, gone touring the countryside of Spain, partied all night in Amsterdam, and seen the ultramodern buildings in Tokyo, Japan.

In all those travels, I witnessed a tremendous display of wealth etched on every picturesque architectural edifice, the technological innovations, the vast riches of the oceans, the smell of commerce in busy retails stores, stock markets, supermarkets, wet markets, and even the black market.

Been there done that.

But just when I thought I have seen enough, my whole point of view changed when I got to Davao City, Philippines.

Behind the city's economic developments, I was wretched to see some groups of children and women with half-clad babies in their arms ply the streets daily to beg for alms under all weather conditions. They wear no slippers, no shoes. Their skin is dark brown probably from too much sun exposure. Their hair is usually auburn and golden brown, which I later learned from my readings, was primarily due to the effects of malnutrition. I seriously thought it was from being sun-baked.

I found out that these people belong to an indigenous tribe called Sama Dilaut commonly known as Badjao in the Philippines – a minority tribe widely regarded to as water-dwelling, they are coined as sea gypsies.

Their lives revolve around the riches of the ocean. It's their main source of food and livelihood, their proverbial territory.

The Badjao are also called sea nomads due to their vast history of living in boathouses and making the ocean their "homeland" where they roamed and lived freely without borders.

Presently, they live a semi-nomadic lifestyle in this part of the planet. They spend days out in the ocean to fish and come home to their stilt houses along the coastlines that keep them close to their marine paradise.

The Badjao are known for their exemplary diving skills and catching fish with their spears. The ocean is their home, their kingdom.

So why were they now proliferating the streets begging for food and money?

And why, in the face of their seemingly enigmatic culture and history, have they been perceived as outcasts, uncivilized, dirty and lazy by modern society?

BOOK TWO
Third World

Chapter 1
My First Sight of the Philippine Badjao

*The **Badjaos** are popularly known as the "Sea Gypsies" of the Sulu and Celebes seas. They are traditionally boat dwellers whose religion is a form of ancestor worship mixed with varying degree of Islamic practice. The term "Badjao" is a Malay-Borneo word which connotes "man of the seas" or Orang Laut in Bahasa Melayu.*- WikiPilipinas

I gasped as I saw three little Badjao boys and two young mothers clutching their babies brave the busy streets and reinvent the meaning of beating the red light in an effort to collect a few coins from motorists. The boys could be around 7 – 10 years old based on their height, unless their growth was stunted due to malnutrition. The young mothers could be well in their teens.

Nonetheless, it could be their siblings they were carrying, or close relatives. Seriously they were putting the poor babies in danger and it was hard to watch. One may think they were deliberately using the infants as props to look more pitiful and gain more handouts. Should this suspicion be true, that's an appalling display of exploitation.

The question was: Were they even aware that they were putting the babies in harm's way? Or could it be that they were plainly ignorant about the perils of their actions?

Could it be that just because the practice is acceptable in their tribe, they thought it was morally right and proper everywhere? What if they only needed to be aware that there was more to life than begging, especially with infants?

What if they only needed to be educated so they would become useful to the society instead of being branded as parasites for generations?

These thoughts hounded me since day one.

I observed that most people now depict the Badjaos as begging parasites instead of fishermen who, for hundreds of years, have co-existed with the ocean without harming its biodiversity --- People who used to be known for their diving skills, able to stay underwater for as long as five minutes without diving gadgets except for a pair of wooden goggles --- People who dive for pearls and sometimes sell them still attached to their shells, you can be sure they're authentic.

The Badjao kids stamped their palms and peeked through car windows and public utility vehicles at the stop sign. Sometimes they picked up coins that were hastily dropped by last-minute Good Samaritans who must have debated with themselves first whether to give or not.

While some people may have nothing to give, some may have different philosophies and avenues to help the less fortunate instead of handing dole outs directly to the begging Badjaos.

Society has tagged them as lazy and dependent, it's quite a challenge to convince the locals otherwise.

To many, they are pests to society for they reject to help themselves. Do they really? Or are they just devoid of better options?

The reasons for turning a blind eye on this tribe are numerous and deeper than it meets the eye. It could take a different book altogether.

It is also important to note that the country has an anti-mendicancy law which prohibits begging and giving alms. This law recognizes that "mendicancy breeds crime, creates traffic hazards, endangers health, and exposes mendicants to indignities and degradation."

Apparently this law was aimed at preventing "the exploitation of infants and children through mendicancy and provide rehabilitative services for those already exploited or in immediate danger of exploitation."

This law, which also protects children from being exploited by their parents or unscrupulous individuals to earn money, sends a message from the government that good Samaritans should channel their donations to legitimate organizations to better the lives of the less fortunate.

I recognize that generosity can potentially be counter-productive when it supports and encourages mendicancy.

Sometimes there's a thin line between fixing and snowballing a problem.

There are certain times when noble motives don't suffice without proper planning and execution.

But could these people's empty stomachs really wait for some long-awaited sustainable programs to be put into place for them? Are the present programs enough to equip them with practical skills they could use to earn a decent living and live among the majority without fear of discrimination? Are the available programs enough to provide these people with basic necessities like proper shelter, food, potable water and health services?

If there were livelihood opportunities available for them, would these people not grab them? If there were opportunities for learning and development without them spending a peso they would rather spend on food, would they not grab them? Would society stop mocking them while they try to live harmoniously with the rest of the world?

The way I see it, there is no hard and fast rule in giving this indigenous tribe a fair fight. It could take a lifetime and would involve all sectors of society as stakeholders. No band-aid solution here.

There have been a number of times when the street beggars including the Badjaos were "swept clean" and apprehended by authorities in keeping with the said law. But most of the time, the law was not implemented. If it was, I would have been slapped with a P20 fine already every time I handed a coin to my Badjao friends on the street. And they would have been fined as much asP500 or slept in jail for up to two years! That's not the kind of board and lodging I was hoping for them to have.

The kids, being kids, were either oblivious of the dangers around them or it was purely the power of hunger and necessity that drove them to be fearless.

Did they really want to be beggars because they were lazy? Or were they displaced from their livelihood sources due to hostility?

Chapter 2
The Encounter that Launched Lunches, Friendships, and Changed My Life Forever!

"Get away from me!" I yelled at the three unrelenting Badjao girls whom after I've given them a few coins kept following me on the street asking for more.

They didn't seem to understand that beggars can't be choosers or perhaps they just refused to be dictated by social norms, much less conform to them. After all, they were touted as social outcasts so why should they care, right?

They probably knew only one thing: that their stomachs were empty and the P5 coins I gave each of them were not enough to buy a few grains of rice for their respective families. Commercial rice of decent quality by the way costs around P38 per kilo and up (approximately 90 US cents at an exchange rate of 42 pesos to a dollar).

The girls continued to follow me around with their bare feet seemingly unmindful of the scorching hot pavement. Maybe they have developed too much callous on their soles that they could no longer feel the heat and sharp bumps beneath their feet.

Their persistence would shame any salesman.

How could I ignore them when they were relentless in tugging at my conscience until I gave in and reached for my pocket in search of some decent amount to spare? The problem was they were tugging at my shirt too and kept poking at my arms. They unceremoniously stretched out their empty hands towards me with their sorry-looking eyes.

"Get your dirty hands off me!" This time, I raised my voice loudly. I had become very angry by this point. "Go away!"

What happened next caught me off guard. One of girls then asked the other two to give her the coins and she then attempted to return them to me. One of the coins dropped to the ground into a puddle of water and I reached down to retrieve it. In doing so my hands got pretty dirty. The girl then reached out for the hem of her rainbow colored *malong*, a traditional "tube skirt" pulled up to her waist. The *malong* may also be used as a blanket, a turban, a hammock, practically anything within the stretch of one's creativity and necessity. She used the cleanest part of the cloth to meticulously wipe the dirt and grime off my hands.

When she was finished she just looked at me and smiled.

It was at that very instant that I realized that I was wrong for so many years. Not just wrong for living the way I had up until that point, but wrong for believing I was a saved, Born Again Christian. At that very moment it was like there was nothing or anyone else around. I couldn't even hear the sound of traffic passing by. It was a very powerful moment.

I immediately went to the room I was staying in and with tears rolling I thanked God for preserving my life until I was able to know the truth. I immediately knew that had I died prior to that meeting with the Badjao children I would have spent eternity in Hell.

The following weekend these same three children were outside the church begging as they always have. Upon seeing them I said "Come with me. Let's talk over lunch," using the most understandable hand signals I could think of.

Motorists and passersby must have had an amusing show of charade as I flung my arms in the air and mimicked eating with my bare hands before those colorfully-clad kids at the busy sidewalk.

Here in this part of town, you don't see many people stopping by to converse with members of this tribe. Doing so, especially if you're a foreigner, would make heads turn. But come to think of it, it's the same banana anywhere in the world. How often do you see people spend time chit-chatting with street beggars in the US or someplace else?

People just give and go.

The look of reluctance and distrust were evident on the kids' faces. I couldn't blame them. The man who was yelling at them and was shooing them away just a few days earlier is now inviting them to lunch. They probably thought I was psychotic. I later found out that it's not easy to gain these people's trust, which is quite understandable for any oppressed group or individual for that matter. You would put up a wall around you if you have been a constant target of ridicule and discrimination.

Finally, their empty stomachs pushed their feet to move along and follow me when I trudged to the direction of a nearby eatery.

I placed my hands on the table as if was laying down my cards. Three innocent-looking kids whose clothes and bodies looked and smelled unwashed for days, were looking at me across the table. Their hours of exposure to smog and dirt while toiling the streets barefoot have riddled them with specs of dirt from head to toe.

"How could I communicate with these kids who couldn't speak nor understand English and whose dialect I've never known from Adam?" Such was my dilemma.

"My name is Joseph. What are yours?" was the best start I could muster. Was it my imagination when I saw the girl's face light up and her eyes go moist as she slowly uttered her name?

"CAR-MI-NA," she said, carefully stressing every syllable as if she was talking to Tarzan. She pointed her finger to herself as she uttered her name. I was surprised that she could understand English. I have gone to other places in the world where even the schooled people could hardly understand and converse in English.

Carmina's facial expression gave out a hint of pride and joy that somebody outside her tribe finally took the time to sit her down and cared to ask about her name. I must have awoken some deep-seated longing in her to be treated with respect despite the family and tribe she was born into.

One by one, they told me their names. Carmina. Almeda. Sonja. Shame I made them so primitive in my mind when I braced to hear names that would fit more in the category of tongue twisters for me.

"HOW --- OLD --- ARE --- YOU--- KIDS?" I asked rather loudly and slowly, hoping that they would understand my alien language better that way. All three of them looked at me quizzically then flashed innocent smiles at me, then at each other, then back at me. Were they amused that I was talking like an idiot? Or were they not comprehending me at all?

Sigh. This was going to be hard after all.

"Look, I'm sorry that I yelled at you last week," I continued in a pace much slower than I would usually talk, "but you have to learn some manners and respect other people's spaces."

I was unsure if my point was being understood but what else could I really do? I have never been too good with sign language so it wasn't a better option at that point. Besides, the messages that I wanted to get across were too abstract for charades, at least for my standards.

The kids could easily read me wrong if I tried to communicate through body movements, not to mention that it would make me look too comical in public. I had to take a chance on words.

The kids looked like they were listening intently so that was at least motivating.

We ate lunch together that day.

Later conversations revealed that Carmina came from a big family, Carmina being the oldest child. To my rough estimate, she's probably 17 or younger. Carmina married young (though she couldn't tell how old she was when she tied the knot, I could tell from her wedding picture that she was definitely a minor, maybe around 14 at the time). She now has a baby that is probably one year old (she's not sure how old her baby is either). She has 8 other siblings (there had been 10 kids in the family until one died from an illness) and most of them beg around too.

They beg as a means to help bring food on the table while their father goes fishing and their mother sells used shoes. That lunch with Carmina, Almeda and Sonya spawned another lunch and another until it became a regular Sunday affair.

The girls and some of their friends and family would wait on me outside the church I went to every Sunday thereafter. Sometimes they were already there even before the service started. I always admired their punctuality despite not knowing how to use a watch. Amazing how they are able to tell time with accuracy without looking at a clock.

In no time, words spread among their tribe members and the number of kids I had to feed every Sunday snowballed into 10, 30 and just recently, 75. Who knows how many would show up the next weekend?

With our group getting bigger by the week, it was getting harder for me to find us a place to eat. The big fast-food chain we went to refused to let the kids in. The guard squirted my Badjao friends with water to keep them out. We had to eat our chicken meals at the sidewalk while sitting on the hot pavement. Occasionally we had sundaes too.

Curious passersby sometimes took pictures of us as if we were zoo animals. There's no telling where our faces may have been posted in this day of social media. They could have been plastered all over facebook, youtube, instagram, or various other websites both obscure and popular without my knowledge. I may never find out.

But wherever our photos might have reached, I hope that the message of sharing, hope and compassion went with them too.

Over the course of one year, my friends have manifested positive changes in the way they behave in public and among themselves. Before, they used to wrestle against each other at the sight of food. Once the food packs were served, they would run towards them in frenzy like hungry cheetahs going for the kill. As soon as they snatched their shares of lunch, they would disperse to all directions. No thank yous, no goodbyes, no looking back.

In a blink of an eye, all that was left was me and some remnants of the kids' lunch, if there were some of them who decided to eat at the area.

Over time, they learned to act in a civilized manner. Well…almost. The food fights lessened or at least became manageable.

Carmina's leadership gradually unraveled before us. She would organize the kids to line up properly to get food. Sometimes Carmina and I would end up not having food for ourselves when the number of kids swelled and the budget was tough.

One time, my money was barely enough to feed 13 children and myself. Just as we were about to eat, one kid came running late. All that was left in my pocket was taxi fare to get home. I could not shell out another P70 or $1.75 for an additional chicken meal. So I gave him mine.

The smallest Badjao girl, probably 7 years old, saw that I had nothing to eat. She tore off a chunk of her fried chicken and laid it on the bare table before me. The rest of the kids followed suit. Soon enough I had more than enough chicken for lunch. Who would think that these little "savages" have bigger hearts than some "civilized" people?

I have also noticed that not all of them would consume all their food. Many of them would have left-overs that they carried along as they left for home. Perhaps they didn't like the food?

Eventually, the kids learned to pick up their own trash before crushing me with hugs and bidding me goodbye. They also learned to say thank you. I figured that these kids who used to act like savages were teachable after all.

Hope is not lost for this tribe. Education is the key.

"I will get these kids to school no matter what," was a conviction I made to myself.

I also found out why they sometimes ran away with their meals. They wanted to share their food with their respective families.

One piece of chicken and a cup of rice. It was barely enough for one child. Yet sharing food with the family, no matter how tiny, seemed to bring my Badjao friends so much joy.

How they are able to contain themselves from eating the tasty lunch they had in their tiny hands was beyond me. For kids, it would probably take a lot of self-control, not to mention that they don't get to eat this good pretty often.

While many kids in first world countries would probably sulk at a small chunk of meat prepared for them at the table, these Badjao kids saved the best parts for their parents and siblings at home. If I were put in the same situation as a kid, I would devour the food myself in no time.

The kids' transformation hadn't been easy. It took over a year before they behaved a little bit better than my first few encounters with them.

There was a time when about 30 Badjao of all ages ganged up on me for alms at the side of the street. It only started with three kids that I gave coins to. To my horror, other members of the tribe suddenly appeared from nowhere, crowding in on me with their arms unanimously stretched towards me. I was practically overwhelmed.

I have been warned by locals before that once you give coins to some of them, the rest of the group would hover around you and suck you dry and that's pretty much what happened on this day.

My then fiancé did not fully support my idea of charity at first. To her, the Badjaos are poor because they choose to be poor. They simply refuse to work. She believed the Badjaos content themselves with living out of other people's hard-earned money. And she was not alone in that perception. I found more people having the same point of view as hers than mine.

Chapter 3
The Exodus

The blue sky was a massive canvas painted with white cottony clouds and cheerful streaks of yellow and orange emanating from the morning sun.

The sun's golden rays plowed into the clear blue sea, illuminating the exuberant seabed and revealing the fertile marine world right below Tenani Mukadam's fishing boat. Schools of fish swam over colorful anemones, corals, and other marine species that extensively loaded the waters of Sulu with life.

Tenani and 10 other Sama fishermen in five separate boats have caught enough fish and clams to sell for the day. The ocean has again rewarded them with its bounty.

Tenani told his fellow fishermen that he would go ahead. He couldn't wait to make money out of his fresh harvests so he could feed his family back home. They could now be waiting on him at the shore.

His friends waved him goodbye with smiles on their faces. It was a happy, rewarding day.

That was the last time Tenani saw some of them alive. Shortly after he left, his friends fell victims to the notorious masked men who have been attacking the helpless Badjao fishermen at sea. The modern-day heavily-armed pirates allegedly attacked the fishermen, ransacked their boats and took their harvests including their motors. Those who resisted got shot. Some were forced to dive into the water.

The terror in the seas of Sulu gripped the Badjao fishermen for many years. Some called it ethnic persecution. It pushed many members of the Sama tribe to search for safer waters across the country where they could fish and live in peace.

And that included Tenani's family.

Crowding his entire family together in his fishing boat, Tenani sailed towards the Southern part of Mindanao until they finally anchored along the coastlines of Davao City.

That was decades ago. A year that Tenani has long forgotten but the memories were etched in his memory like it was yesterday.

No one in Tenani's family could remember the exact year of their exodus from Zamboanga to Davao. They could not read calendars. They do not even know their ages and birthdays. That explains why Carmina, Bobby and Donita could not give me their ages when I asked. Not that they did not understand my question. They simply did not know the answers.

Since the migration, Tenani's family has grown to three generations. He is now a grandfather of 11 and great grandfather of 16 kids.

It was his grandchildren and great grandchildren that I met on the streets of Davao that became my first Badjao friends.

Chapter 4
Typhoon Bopha Devastation

December 4, 2012. Mindanao was devastated by the biggest and probably the worst typhoon that hit the island. Typhoon Bopha flattened hundreds of miles of farmlands in Davao Oriental and Compostela Valley which left more than a thousand people dead and close to nine hundred missing plus over two thousand injured. Estimated damage was 1 billion dollars, making it the costliest typhoon to hit the country, according to news reports.

Tara, a friend whom I had just recently ventured into a small business with, and I decided to conduct our own small relief operations.

In between demanding schedules and other pressures of starting a business, Tara and I managed to squeeze in charity work.

I communicated with my friends in the US about the cause while Tara appealed to her local friends for help of any kind. Our main goal was to send relief goods to Baganga, a remote municipality in the province of Davao oriental that was badly hit by the catastrophe. Tara and I have been there before when we made a writing project with a government agency.

The family of farmers that we met during that project was the very reason why I pushed all buttons to gather needed resources. I couldn't get them off my mind. Did they even survive?

The pressure took a toll on Tara who struggled to spread herself too thin between managing the business and the charity campaign. We ended up fighting almost every day as our trip schedules kept stalling due to insufficient funds.

It wasn't easy pooling in donations. In fact, it was frustrating. I was getting mad hearing from my friends and family in the US that they barely have enough money for themselves so they couldn't help, only to see them bragging about their excessive lifestyles in social networking sites --- dining in expensive restaurants, partying all night, etc.

For me, flamboyant display of wealth is reflective of bad character.

I became a bitter person. I began deleting friends on Facebook which was the only platform that connected us. I cut ties with family members who were greedy and self-absorbed. I was angry to the point of yelling at Tara when I pushed her to help fast-track our relief mission.

"We can't give what we don't have!" Tara reasoned in response to my persistence in giving aid to our farmer friends. The cost of transportation alone was almost $180 and we didn't even have that.

We were both angered by the reports that relief goods were not reaching the communities affected. Food and medical supplies were scarce and people were dying. A lot of roads were impassable, making the relief and rescue operations even harder.

In the end, we were able to come up with 10 sacks of goods composed of uncooked rice, noodles, canned goods, medicines and used clothing from friends and family. With very little money, we could only do so much.

We traveled in zigzag but fairly safe roads for 8 hours from Davao City. We had to take the longest route since the other roads were not accessible due to landslides.

"The first day I drove around here after the disaster, I saw the people walking aimlessly like zombies," said our hired driver.

"The people were covered in mud. Some were shocked. Some were crying. Some were looking for lost family members.

"It was a scene that one could never forget in his lifetime," the driver said.

The driver was referring to his experience in New Bataan, a low-lying municipality in Compostela Valley that was partly buried in mud and rocks that came cascading from the wall of mountains surrounding it. The chilling mudslide wiped out the banana plantations, homes and other man-made structures in the poor valley. The once-abundant farmers were reduced to being beggars in the streets.

For miles and miles, our views of the countryside were a shattering demonstration of the forces of nature.

It was the worst natural disaster I have ever seen in my whole life, in all the places I've traveled to.

Coconut trees were uprooted as though they were pulled from the ground by some gigantic trolls. Houses were either flattened or overturned. We saw a wooden house along the highway that was obviously blown by the strong winds upside down, its roof was on the ground. Some of the more fortunate houses stood firm but the roofs and some walls were gone.

Residents walked around hoping to chance upon relief operations initiated by all sectors, including individuals like us. Many of them lost not only their livelihood but more painfully, some members of their families and friends. How worse could it get?

And with most man-made structures almost gone, how could we find the family of farmers we came here for? We weren't even sure if they were still alive. We were just taking our chances.

Finally in the midst of the rubble, we found the family and yes, I was relieved to know that they survived. However, they lost some relatives who refused to evacuate their house before the typhoon lashed out.

They were surprised to see us and could not contain their joy.

"We were just talking about you last night," said Rudy, the head of the family excitedly. The warm welcome was very humbling. It was like being reunited from long lost friends even though this was only the second time we ever saw each other and talked. I don't know but since the day I met this family several months ago, I have already considered them very good friends.

"We lost our farm. We lost our hopes. Then we wondered, what if you came over?" There was happiness in Rudy's voice.

"We were hoping you would, but we never expected it," his wife sad. "And now you both are here! It's like a dream."

I wish we were able to do more. Being there with very limited resources was a bit depressing. Hearing the people's plights and unable to do something about them felt like daggers to my chest. The goods we brought were too little to augment their ordeal.

"We get more help from private companies and individuals like you as well as from non-government organizations than the government," my farmer friend said, which was echoed by random people we talked to as we walked around the area.

Sad and infuriating.

The municipality's roofless hospital only had one doctor who hadn't even had the chance to go home since the typhoon.

"I don't know what my house looks like now or if it's still there," said the female doctor. "I have to do my duty as a physician. There's no one else here to take my place."

Time and again, medical volunteers from various organizations came to help but the lack of medical supplies and equipment in the hospital vis-à-vis the actual need was apparent.

The place didn't even look like anything resembling a hospital. If not for the cloth banner bearing the sign "Medical Mission," we would have been clueless that it was the hospital we were looking for to donate the few boxes of medicine we brought.

It was a one-story structure, about the size of an average 4-bedroom house in a middle-class subdivision in the US. Looking from the outside, the structure was in ruins. It looked abandoned. Most of the roof was gone. Upon entering the small building, puddles of rainwater could be seen on the floor. The risk of slipping was high but apparently no one took the time to clear out the mess.

Most of the residents were still in shock to start rebuilding their lives again, much more clean up their small hospital. The walls were partly damaged. Only the aching wails of ill babies down the hall gave an indication that there was life in that building.

Older patients awaiting medication quietly sat on the benches and chairs along the damp corridors. On the right wing of the building was a partially broken wall with the painted sign "TB Room" or what was left of it.

While Tara and I intended to go back to Baganga with more medical supplies, food and plants seedlings in the near future, I continued my humble feeding mission for the Badjaos in the city.

That was the only feasible thing I could do for the moment.

With the Badjao people, the face of depression I saw and felt at the typhoon-devastated areas was somehow replaced with joy. The Badjaos' happy disposition in the face of poverty and nothingness was contagious.

Chapter 5
The Badjao Village

I wanted to have a clearer understanding of my Badjao friends' way of living so I would know better how to help them.

To do this, I needed to go to their village, know their happiness and predicament, their beliefs and traditions, learn how they live… or get by.

Only when I see things from their perspective will I get to really understand them. Tara calls it immersion. I call it a mission.

Helping these people is now my new calling.

I intended to talk to their community leader and other members of the tribe to gather more insights.

What else constitute their ordinary day apart from begging and fishing? Have they made begging a way of life? Are they really lazy? What kind of houses do they live in? Why don't the kids go to school when public education in this country is free or at least comes with a very little cost?

I asked Carmina if she could take me to her village. It was time to meet the parents.

Carmina took me to their house and introduced me to tens of her family members. God, they were aplenty. Nine siblings (They lost one of their 10 siblings to Dengue), numerous cousins, a few aunts and uncles.

That's when I met Carmina's grandfather, Tenani, who was now incapacitated from the waist down. I was afraid he's been struck by a disease called Barotrauma that some Badjao fishermen acquire after being exposed to "compressor fishing."

This method of fishing is illegal in the country. It uses a compressor (which is sometimes old and rusty as perhaps they can't afford to buy brand new ones) with a plastic tube attached to it, where the Badjao divers breathe from as they plunge into the depths of the ocean to hunt for fish. The risks involved are so high that it could eventually paralyze or kill the ones using it.

Tenani's family was one of the first few Badjaos that settled in that area called Isla Verde which literally translates to Green Island in English.

Ironically, I did not see anything that would justify the name of the place. There were hardly any greens in the village. If there were any plants, they were a bunch of grass sprouting at the street side or a few coconut trees scattered across the supposedly green village.

Instead, the more prominent were the brown and grey wooden shanties and concrete apartments lined up along the partially paved roads going deep into the Badjao village.

Nevertheless, I believe Isla Verde got its name for a reason. Perhaps what used to be a lush vegetation in this area has in recent years been replaced with man-made structures as more and more people settled in.

The coastal village which was initially inhabited solely by members of the Sama tribe is now home to Muslims and Bisayas as well. Tenani said that since their community leader died many years ago, other tribes started to come in and settled in their village.

The absence of a Sama leader in Isla Verde could also be the reason why the entire village is swimming in trash. There is nobody to initiate community clean-up drives, promote proper garbage disposal in every home, or band the tribe members together to fix their wooden walkways.

(Note: While this book was being finished, the government built a concrete walkway from the middle of the Badjao Village leading towards the shoreline.)

My Badjao friends live on stilt houses at the edge of the sea.

The water below the houses are littered with all types of wastes you can imagine, engulfing the once-clear-blue sea bursting with rich marine life like in most parts of the Pacific Ocean.

The path to the Badjao houses was a long and wobbly walk over rickety bamboo strips too narrow for two people (though I was blown to see some members of the tribe easily walk past each other as if they were walking on pavement). The Badjaos' light and generally petite frame makes them agile for those stick walkways.

It was no rocket science to see that the living conditions of the so-called sea gypsies were deplorable. Poor sanitation and personal hygiene make them very susceptible to skin diseases and other health hazards.

Common colds are, well, very common to the Badjao kids. And wiping them off from their noses doesn't look like one of their priorities. Tara had to give out tissue paper before the kids even realized they had something running through their noses that they had to wipe.

Poor supply of potable water is another setback in the Badjao community. They have to buy water from somewhere in the neighborhood for P1 per gallon and tread heavily with them over the long and unsteady bamboo bridge that snaked around the village.

Every step I took over the makeshift bridge came with a throbbing fear that I could fall into the sea of trash anytime.

Since the frail walkway had no side railings to hold on to, I had to reach out to the walls of the nearby stilt houses.

Many times, Carmina and her younger sister Donita reached out their hands to assist me but I feared I could tow them off when I lose balance. I was too big and heavy for them to support.

Tara and I have been informed by some barangay workers that there have been village visitors in the past that were pushed off this very bridge by members of the tribe.

"They push those people who take advantage of them," we were told. We had nothing to worry about in that case. Apparently these people have been exploited many times over by bogus charitable institutions and individuals. These flakes rake in huge funding from well-meaning donors around the world but the money never reached my friends in need. This makes me mad.

Alas, we got to the house of Carmina's parents where eight of her siblings live. Carmina, being married, lives in another Badjao village in the city called Dabsa.

The stilt house was a simple architecture made of various wooden patches. Bamboo slats made up their floors while the walls were a jumbled pattern of matted nipa and cardboard full of gaps and holes. The windows were empty squares with no jalousies or boards to cover them for security or privacy. The door had no shutter. There were no curtains either, just empty sacks of rice pinned against the wall to patch up bigger holes.

Upon entry, we saw their small kitchen. And I mean small like about 2x2 square feet just enough to cook food on the floor from their kerosene stove. There was a small pot and a frying pan lying on the kitchen floor.

Tara and I brought them a thermos, a set of cups and pitcher, a 5-gallon water container, a pail and a basin. We also brought them groceries which we previously thought would last for a week. But having met their large family now, the bags of groceries might just last for less than five days.

Since then I've been bringing them groceries every Tuesday of the week.

Several neighbors, whose houses almost touched the walls of our hosts' house, peered over from their respective windows and waved happily at us while we were inside. Everyone looked happy and friendly.

"Joseph," some of them called out my name.

"Hey! How are you?" I replied. They answered with huge smiles on their faces.

They looked delighted to have someone actually greeting them and talking to them like normal people. Beyond the confines of this village, they are treated as social outcasts. They get frowned upon, mocked, ridiculed, verbally and physically harassed.

They have gotten so used to people being rude to them that they get surprised or elated when someone actually takes time to exchange pleasantries with them.

Their houses have no bathroom.

Carmina's family bathe in one corner of the house that had no partition for a little bit of privacy. There was also a small portion of the floor were they could detach a couple of bamboo slats and squat there when nature calls. The sea of trash below practically served as a floating septic tank. Tenani, whose house was a few meters away from Carmina's parents,' recalled that those waters used to be clear and basking with life where they could see small fishes and other marine animals through gaps of the bamboo strips that made up their floors.

Today, the trash was too much that the saltwater along the Isla Verde coastline is now covered with piles of it. The filth around the village is a smorgasbord of floating and submerged waste materials.

Often times you can smell the filth in the air. The surface of the water is swamped with trash but through a few gaps one could see through the bottom (during low tide) which is also covered with silts.

There is not a single hint of proper garbage disposal being implemented in this village.

Compared to the two other Sama villages in Dabsa and Matina Aplaya (both of which have leaders), Isla Verde pales in the cleanliness and discipline departments.

While I felt sorry for their living conditions, they looked rather cheerful. They seemed to be unmindful of their squalid surroundings. I wasn't sure if that was a good trait or not.

How could they be happy in this terrible swamp of a life? Where do they exhume their laughter from?

My frequent visit to the village gained me some interesting information about them.

While the Badjaos or Sama Dilaut (The word "dilaut" refers to the ocean) train their kids to the aquatic way of life at an early age, it is a myth that they throw their new-born babies into the ocean. That common misconception, which they find silly, never fails to draw out laughter among them.

Apparently, people outside the tribe have had that misconception for many years that even a Filipino movie released in the 70's has that scene of a Badjao baby being thrown into the ocean.

"Would you throw your baby out into the sea?" They would ask you back.

However, some of them throw the placenta, not the baby, into the ocean believing that by doing this, the ocean will protect their child.

These water people worship their dead ancestors. They believe that the dead are capable of watching over them and extending them help from the spirit world.

They believe in spirit mediums in casting out spirits that cause epidemics in the community. To execute this exorcism, they set out a so-called spirit boat to drift into the open sea, away from the village.

Chapter 6
The Learning Center

I decided I would contribute to this community by opening a learning center nearby. And I did. I named it Babina Monare Badjao Learning Center in memory of Carmina's younger sister who died from Dengue. She was in 3rd grade when the supposedly curable illness took her life. Due to the family's financial constraints, she was not given the proper treatment on time.

The learning center sits at the boundary of a Muslim-populated area and the Badjao village. The Badjaos are said to be included under the Muslim groups. Hence, technically, they are Muslims too but with different practices, beliefs and traditions. Despite me knowing that the two groups don't get along well, I pushed through with my plan on having the informal school there due to its proximity to my friends' stilt houses.

When we opened the learning center, Muslim kids pleaded that we take them in. They were eager to learn, in fact, more eager than the Badjao kids.

For the Badjao kids to go to the learning center, we needed to lure them in with free food. We serve lunch every day after classes. We also provide all the learning materials such as books and writing and coloring instruments. This is all on top of their free transportation allowance, since most of them live in the other Badjao village which is 3 rides away by public transportation.

I made sure that the kids wouldn't have any excuse not to go to school. But it also meant bigger daily expenses which I could barely handle, considering that donations were very scarce.

Time and again, I was thankful for old and new friends who stretched their own budgets in order to help me carry out my personal mission.

We took 5 Muslims and 16 Badjaos as our first students. I was hopeful that the two tribes would peacefully co-exist in the classroom.

Bad move.

I raised my hopes too high.

Tension was present every single day in the classroom as kids from the two groups would figure in a brawl. Many times, the Badjao kids told us that they would stop going to class because of the Muslims.

The Muslims complained about the Badjaos hitting them so they hit back. They fought nastily, both physical and verbal.

The two teachers I hired for the school often got caught in the middle. Half the time, they failed to resolve the issues, they only broke the fights.

"Patyon ta mo tanan (I'll kill all of you!)," threatened one of our Muslim students in one of the regular fights in the class.

He was only 8 years old.

The loathing between the two groups as reflected in our own students was probably more than it meets the eye. They could have acquired it from their ancestors.

The disgust and dislike among them is prevalent even when we walk the streets with the Badjaos. Muslim vendors (and I mean full grown men and women) would call the Badjao kids names or say something nasty.

Though I couldn't understand their dialect, I could tell from the Badjaos' upset reaction that the Muslims said something distasteful or provocative. Then they would start retaliating by engaging in a shouting match in public. Yes, with me smacked right in the middle.

I cannot generally say that it's always the Muslims who instigate the trouble. There have been instances that the Badjao kids started the problems too. They are just not too fond of each other.

Most of the time when we asked the kids to stop fighting, the Muslims would easily extend their hand of friendship and say they're sorry. But the Badjaos wouldn't accept their apology nor would they apologize themselves. They can be very unyielding.

But we're talking about kids here ages 5 to 17 so I'm not very surprised if they act like kids. That's the point of educating them so that these behavioral problems would be averted in the future.

To address the growing tension between the two tribes in the class, we ended up relocating the learning center to near the center of the Badjao village and admitted only Badjao students.

Chapter 7
Spear Fishing and Apnea Diving

The Badjaos are excellent divers and fish hunters. I've never known other groups of people who are as comfortable underwater as on land without any breathing equipment.

Although other members of the tribe have been introduced to the illegal and hazardous compressor fishing, many Badjao divers still hunt fish by holding their breath underwater. There are tales that some of them can even walk on the sea floor.

A free diving competition was held during the city's annual festival called the *Kadayawan* (*Kadayawan* means good or lovely as in "*Madayaw na adlaw*" or lovely day).

The grand champion went down as deep as 261 ft.

While we were watching the video of him descending into the dark ocean, we couldn't help but hold our breath. He had nothing but a pair of goggles. There was a long rope that stretched out from one of the organizer's boats at the surface down to hundreds of feet below as part of security measures.

There was hardly any light penetrating the deep water. The darkness was scary enough, more so the depth and the pressure along with it that could easily burst someone's lungs.

Another one was adjudged winner of the static apnea award for staying underwater the longest time at 3 minutes. I don't think I could hold my breath that long under any circumstances.

The Badjaos' inseparable ties with the ocean are enthralling. For hundreds of years the vast ocean has been their refuge and their source of livelihood.

Apart from fishing, they would dive deep for precious pearls.

Sadly, the pearl culture technology crept in and eventually killed the Badjaos' pearl diving business over the years. The pearls are now being farmed and, with the abundance of supply, the pearls have reduced in value.

Apparently, modernization took a toll on the Badjao. I jumped with excitement when Carmina's family invited me and Tara to go fishing with their family one day. "When do we go?" was my overeager reply.

The narrow boat owned by Carmina's parents bobbed briskly as we headed towards the Island City of Samal two days later. The waves were rough. Water splashed on our skin at some point and the youngest passenger on the boat, Almira, was crying. If not for the boat's wide outriggers, I would have worried it would overturn.

Tara, also not a swimmer like me, wanted to buy us floaters and life jackets the night before. We would have looked funny in those colorful rubbers while we were sandwiched by the half-naked Badjao men. But if those rubbers were to save our lives then I wouldn't mind looking funny.

We were joined by seven other members of Carmina's family, mostly male and apparently very good divers. They were going to show us how they fish using their traditional spears.

Tara and I chose to go with the men to fish. It was almost noontime and the sun was hurting our eyes and skin. But the water below us was refreshing. It revealed a rich marine paradise, if I was to judge according to the colorful corals and anemones I saw. But even as the water below us was crystal clear, I never saw any fish big enough for us to hunt and eat.

One hour. We stayed out in the sea for at least this long while the girls of the clan stayed on the shoreline to start cooking rice and their staple food, ground cassava that they call "syanglag." The men went down several times with their spears. At last, one of them caught a medium-sized fish still waggling in the spear. The rest of the catches were sea urchins and oysters.

It was alarming how there was no fish to be found. If that part of the ocean was over fished and the natural pearl business is dead, what else will my Badjao friends do to eke out a living?

No wonder they're forced to beg.

Chapter 8
Of Factions and Rivalry

Since I started the Sunday lunches more than a year ago, my Badjao friends multiplied exponentially. Word spread among the other Badjao village in Dabsa that I was helping Carmina's family and other kids by feeding them on Sundays, providing them with grocery items and other basic necessities likes clothing, medicine and school supplies.

Now everyone wanted to have a piece of me. My expenses ballooned many times over that I was reeling to keep up even with my own bills. I ended up giving more for charity and Tara didn't think it was smart.

"Help yourself first," she'd often say. "Then you can help others."

"No. We should take care of others first and God will take care of us," I said.

I'm not rich and I'm afraid I don't have the capacity to support more kids than I already do at the moment. But how could I say no to the growing number of kids wanting to go to school? These kids, who are often discriminated against by society, understand that education is their way out of poverty and marginalization.

Other Badjaos do not comprehend this though. I tried to persuade many of them to go to school but they bluntly told me they just wanted to beg.

"Why don't you wanna go to school?" I asked.

"Because we don't have money for school," said one of them.

"How about if I pay for your education?"

"We will just beg."

"Why do want to beg?"

"Because we need to buy food."

"Why? Where are your parents?"

"At home."

"Then why don't they work instead of you kids begging?"

"They beg too. We all beg."

"How about if I buy you food, would you go to school and stop begging?"

"No, we won't go to school. We'll just beg."

That was a sad conversation. I never saw that poor girl again.

I realized then that this tribe has deeper problems than poverty. Poverty is merely an effect of a broader and more complex problem. Part of it is their apparent culture of mendicancy that was passed on from generation to generation. It's their unwillingness to advance. It's their own limiting mindset that denies them a chance to rise from their present battles.

The good news is that not all Badjaos share the same paradigm. A lot of them, like the kids who begged me to finance their schooling, have seen the light. It surely helped that the parents of these kids were supportive of their goal to get a formal education.

So how could I say no?

I started bugging my friends for donations to help the kids that are way beyond my financial power to assist.

Thankfully, a number of them wired some money in an instant. We were able to enroll and buy school supplies for the kids who were eager to get educated.

Some of the kids were not registered with the Local Civil Registrar. They have no birth certificates which was a requirement for enrollment. So Tara and I went to the Barangay Hall to get them a barangay certificate in lieu of the birth certificate.

The problem was, the kids nor their parents knew their birthdays and ages. Hence, we invented them. December 25 and February 14. How convenient. Now they have birthdays that they will never forget.

We bought the kids shoes, bags, school uniforms and everything they needed in school. I also provided them with school allowance every week.

When their school requirements were met, they began asking for other things like dresses, t-shirts, shorts, and slippers. Depending on the need, some kids got more assistance than others kids. And this became a problem I did not foresee. Apparently, if things were not distributed equally down to the cent, they get jealous.

This is what Tara has been warning me --- that the kids would eventually breed envy and jealousy among themselves, causing unnecessary rift within the community.

The tension started when I became friends with more kids especially a new girl named Hanora, a 16-year old Badjao. I had high hopes for this girl as she came up to me as smart and rather ambitious.

I paid for Hanora's school requirements and allowances.

There's no tuition to worry about because she's enrolled in a public school. She is currently on 2nd year high school and was easily elected as class president. I could say she has a promising future and I vowed to help her achieve her dreams.

However, Hanora and Carmina have developed some kind of rivalry. From what I understand, Carmina thought that Hanora's family was taking advantage of me and she wasn't happy about it. Hanora, on the other hand, belies this allegation. She believes that Carmina hates it when I help others.

Two big factions were formed and ended up in a shouting match at the side of the street during one of our Sunday lunches. I was surprised that we weren't arrested for public disturbance.

It took a while before we got the warring sides to sit down and talk properly and calmly. We did not go home that day without patching up the conflict.

But that wasn't the only issue that sprang from jealousy. I found out that the parents of some of the kids beat them up whenever they failed to get as much help from me as with the other kids I'm helping. Once I give one child a t-shirt, they should have one too or else their parents would scold them and hit them.

I am seriously considering changing my way of helping if it hurts the kids more than it helps them.

Maybe Tara was right in her belief that instead of giving individual dole-outs, we should organize long-term medical and dental missions, community-wide feeding projects, clean-up drives, and a sustainable livelihood project that would benefit more families. That should stop the jealousy in the tribe.

But considering that operating the learning center alone is getting a huge chunk off my already bleeding wallet, these other programs would definitely be a much bigger challenge for me.

Chapter 9
The Runaway Badjao

"Hanora is missing?" I asked Hanora's mom again to make sure I heard it correctly.

Hanora's mom was crying helplessly as she recounted how she and her daughter had a petty fight the night before she disappeared.

Alarm bells rang in my head. What if she got kidnapped? A couple of days ago, she told me of a foreigner who asked her a lot of personal questions --- where she lives, her age, what she does for a living, etc. He gave her his cell phone number so she could contact him anytime. She didn't know what his interest about her was.

I got the guy's number from Hanora and contacted him. I needed to see what he was up to and made sure he was not a threat to my Badjao friend. I met with the guy downtown and from our conversations, he seemed alright.

I had no idea that on that same day that I met with the said foreigner, Hanora had disappeared.

Hanora's mom had no clue where her daughter went. But she was afraid she ran away with her boyfriend. That is probably better than being kidnapped by a stranger.

If the two actually eloped, their tradition restricts the mother from looking for her own daughter. It has to be the boy's parents who should find the couple if they want to bring them back home.

I can't believe that in this day and age, these people remain prisoners to this tradition which, to my own point of view, is a blatant disregard to the rights of the women in their tribe. While I respect their customs and traditions, I am appalled that these very aspects are the ones keeping them from thriving in the modern world.

Badjao women have little freedom in choosing their husbands. That freedom and privilege usually lies in the hands of the men's parents. Once the parents of the male have decided who they want to be their son's bride is, both the son and the chosen bride would have to accept it as their fate.

The boy's family would have to pay dowry to the girl's family before the marriage is executed.

In the case of Hanora who apparently ran away with her boyfriend, her mother would need to buy her back if she refuses to allow her daughter to marry. Sounds like ransom money to me.

Hanora's mom would rather spend a fortune to bring back her daughter, although I don't really think she has a lot to give. A fortune for her could be a penny for a lot of people I know. She dreads the day that she would see her daughter going through the very same life she went through when she followed their tradition.

She prefers that her daughter would finish her studies and change the course of her future. If she fails to show up in class any longer, she'll be dropped out.

This wasn't the first time Hanora's eloped. Her mom has bought her back in the past when she ran away the first time with her first husband. And her mom is keen on taking her back again even if it means a lot of money, just to give her daughter a better chance in life.

There's no need for annulment in their tribe. They don't have their marriages registered with the government in the first place.

I vowed to take Hanora back to her mom.

For several days, I searched high and low for Hanora in the places we usually meet up when we go shop for her personal and school needs. I went to the usual spot on our usual schedule. I was hoping that the shopping and the weekly allowance would lure her into showing up. I patiently waited.

But Hanora never came.

Chapter 10
Learning from the Unschooled

Sad but true, my Badjao friends are demoralized everywhere --- even in school where they are supposed to learn not just academics but also proper social behavior, among others.

Unfortunately, the formal learning institutions which are supposed to be their second homes, do not offer a friendly environment for them. They are looked down upon, laughed at, not taken seriously by schoolmates and even by some educators.

Carmina's younger brother, Bobby, who I sent to first grade, was humiliated by his own teacher in class. He needed to rush to the restroom but the teacher didn't allow him to go. Bobby couldn't hold his bowels any longer and pooped in his pants. Worse, the teacher humiliated him further by reprimanding him while the whole class was laughing. He never set foot in school again after that incident.

Shouting "Badjao" at them is tantamount to bullying, as the term Badjao has become degrading. Some of my friends were forced to drop from school due to discrimination and bullying. Their only fallback to continuous learning are the informal Badjao learning centers around their communities, like the one I started.

But despite the daily grind they need to surmount, some of them choose to thrive. My Badjao friends, Siva, Jairus, Princess, are now in secondary and primary levels. They continue to fight mockery and poverty.

I admire their resilience.

The Badjaos are people with simple joys, simple pleasures. They are happy with a new pair of slippers. They are ecstatic with a cheap T-shirt, or a lunch pack from a local fast-food restaurant.

A stark contrast from the world I know back in the US. If people think they're poor because they live paycheck to paycheck or can't afford to eat out in restaurants as often as they want or buy the latest gadgets and new shoes and bags, they don't realize how fortunate they still are compared to most people. They have roofs over their heads and enough food inside their fridges. They have soft beds to sleep on and cars to drive. Yet, some of them aren't happy.

In contrast, my Badjao friends are lucky if they get to eat three times a day. They walk around barefoot unless they save enough to buy slippers. If they prioritize slippers and clothes, they would sacrifice food. If they go out fishing in some parts of the ocean, they have chances of getting robbed and killed by pirates. If they fish in the safer waters, chances are, fish are scarce. Yet, they always find several reasons to be happy. They're happy to share resources with their family, even a small chunk of fried chicken. They do things together as a family and I think that's what makes them strong.

Sometimes when I come home to my apartment, I feel guilty for all the material things I have, thinking that my Badjao friends' homes are almost bare even with necessities.

But even in nothingness, they exude contentment and joy. One Badjao kid named Amelita, around 9 years old, proudly showed me their house one day. She climbed up the wooden stairs and upon reaching the doorway, stretched out her arms like a cheerleader ending a grand presentation. Her house was no bigger than a bedroom. No appliances, no furniture. But she proudly showed me her beloved treasure --- her tiny wooden box of clothes.

Indeed, this beautiful country of 7,107 islands on the Western edge of the Pacific Ocean is an archipelago that holds a plethora of resilient and happy people. People with admirable positivity, they could manage to smile even in the midst of natural calamities and poverty. They don't begrudge the government for seeming to forget them. They strive to survive in the harsh world.

I don't want to natter about how society should stop treating my Badjao friends as pests or people who will never amount to anything.
.
But I believe that if one cannot or do not want to help someone, at least he or she should not try to put them down or make their lives even harder.

Despite being ostracized, they go through life in high spirits. They are peace-loving and gentle people. They would rather move from one place to another to avoid conflicts as much as they can. The ocean has become their refuge.

I hope to see my Badjao friends finally experiencing a sense of belongingness in a land where they are treated equally and humanely by modern society.

Maybe the better future that I long for my Badjao friends to have will not happen within my lifetime. Maybe I would long be dead before society would change the way they perceive and interact with these sea gypsies.

What's important is, more people are getting informed about their plight. More people are starting to care. More people are starting to help.

I believe that little acts of kindness will somehow get little rippling effects until it covers more mileage and helps transform lives for the better… one Badjao at a time.

Revisiting Book Two, Chapter Two: The Encounter that Launched Lunches, Friendships, and Changed My Life Forever!

Many people ask me why I have decided to dedicate my life to helping the Badjao and the answer is quite simple. God used them to show me what going to church and listening to countless sermons never could.

In August of 1983 at the age of 15 I asked Jesus into my heart following an evangelistic crusade which visited my hometown in North Carolina and for years afterward I attended various churches of different denominations which continued to assure me that I was "saved" at that crusade in August of 1983.

However; despite being a "Christian", I lived a selfish and reckless life (I will spare all the ugly details). This started in high school, continued during my time in the military and for the many years that followed. All this time I believed that if something were to happen to me that I would be "OK". After all I was going to church and I had invited Jesus into my heart long before.

While I had done some good for others from time to time during my life, for the most part it was about me. That is until a trip I took half way around the world to the island of Mindanao located in the southern Philippines in 2011.

My primary reason for visiting Mindanao was a simple toothache. I had been talking online with a friend I had met on a Christian site for over a year and had always wanted to visit her, but the expense of the trip was too much for my budget. An off and on toothache finally got to the point to where it was becoming unbearable and it forced me to go to the dentist. During that visit to the dentist I learned that I was going to need to get not one, but two root canals and crowns. One of course for the tooth that was bothering me and also one for a tooth on the opposite side. The cost to do this was going to run about $4,000.

Ironically the friend I had been talking with online was renting a room from a dentist so naturally I asked about this procedure and was told that it could be done there in the Philippines for around $500. Once I heard this I decided to check prices for airfare and lodging and found that I could get the dental work done there for far less even with the travel expenses included and it would also allow me to meet my friend in one shot with change to spare. After all, why should I help pay for my dentist to have a vacation in a far away tropical paradise when I could use my hard earned money to do so myself?

It was during this visit that I meet members of a people group called the Badjao. The Badjao are a water based tribe and traditionally they live on the bounties of the sea. They are an animistic tribe for the most part, however; they do have some Islamic influence since they originate from the Muslim regions of Southeast Asia. Due to conflict, piracy, and lack of opportunity, many Badjao have left their ancestral waters and traveled to larger cities far removed from these hardships in search of a better life. Unfortunately most find that the urban areas have little to offer them and many are forced to begging in the streets as a means to survive.

My friend attended a church in the city proper of Davao and each Sunday there would be a group of mostly young Badjao, teenagers and children, standing in front of the church building begging for coins. To be honest I didn't like the Badjao at first, not many people do. They are known for having have poor hygiene, lack proper manors, and could be very aggravating especially when they are in dire need of money. But even then, each Sunday I would make sure I had enough five peso coins to give out to each of these Badjao beggars. I would hand them a coin, they would always say thank you, and then move along to the next prospect.

My trip would last for four weeks and it was on the final weekend of attending church that something out of the ordinary occurred. I gave the begging Badjaos each a coin as I always had, but this time rather than walk away, three young girls began to follow my friend and I as we walked from the church towards the city center to get something to eat. Two of the girls were in their teens, and the youngest was probably around seven years old.

The three girls continued to follow us with their bare feet despite the pavement being scorching hot from the afternoon sun. I guess they had been doing so for so long that they had become immune to the pain.

We tried our best to ignore them as we walked, but when the youngest of the three girls tugged at my shirt, I had no choice but to acknowledge them.

"Get your dirty hands off me!" I said quite loudly. I had become very upset at this point. "Go away! I gave you money already!"

What happened next caught me completely off guard. The oldest of the three girls asked the other two to give her the coins I had given them earlier. She then attempted to return the three five peso coins to me. As she handed them to me, one of the coins slipped through my fingers and dropped into a puddle of water. I reached down to retrieve the coin and in doing so my hands got pretty dirty. The girl then reached out for the hem of her rainbow colored malong, a traditional "tube skirt" she had pulled up to her waist. A malong can also be used as a blanket, hammock, baby carrier, practically anything within the stretch of one's creativity and necessity.

The girl then used the cleanest part of the cloth to meticulously wipe the dirt and grime off my hands and once finished, she just looked at me and smiled. The three Badjao girls then turned and walked away.

At that very moment it was like there was nothing or anyone else around. I couldn't even hear the sound of traffic passing by. I didn't even notice that my friend had slipped away moments earlier and continued up the street without me. It was as if someone had slammed me to the pavement and I could see my old self lying lifeless on the ground. It was a very powerful and life changing moment.

It was also at that very instant that I realized that I had been wrong for so many years. Not just wrong for living the way I had up until that point, but wrong for believing I was saved, wrong for believing that I was a Christian! I immediately knew without a doubt that had I died prior to that encounter with the three young Badjao girls, I would have spent an eternity separated from God.

Needless to say, I left my old self lying there in the street that day. I would return to the room I was staying in, and with tears rolling down my face, thank God for preserving my life until that moment; thank God for using those three Badjao girls to show me the truth.

It's truly amazing how God works sometimes. It took these three three children from a pagan tribe half way around the world to show me what a lifetime of going to church, countless pastors, Sunday school classes, and even my own Christian parents could not. And while my salvation comes only through Jesus Christ and the sacrifice He made for us, God used the Badjao to reveal this to me. It's for this reason that I have committed the rest of my life to helping the Badjao, because the way I see it, I owe them a debt that can never be repaid.

Appendix
Badjao Outreach

Badjao Outreach, Inc., a North Carolina Registered nonprofit, was founded in 2012 and incorporated in 2016.

Its founder, Joseph Zanetti Jr, recognized the plight of the Badjao tribe in Davao City which is located on the island of Mindanao in the southern Philippines while visiting in 2011.

The Badjaos that are found in Davao City are known as sea gypsies and were formally boat dwelling people. They originated from Zamboanga, Basilan, Jolo and Tawi Tawi which make up the Sulu Archipelago in Mindanao. The Badjaos are the poorest and most marginalized ethnic group in Southeast Asia.

What started out as a simple feeding program with a small number of children has since grown into an organization which provides sponsorships for children to enroll in public schools, as well as a learning center which provides both literacy and basic skills for the children and young adults. It also provides livelihood and training programs which enable older members of the tribe to earn a sustainable income for their families.

THE BADJAO*

The name is spelled in various ways: *"Badjao," "Badyaw,"* or *"Bajau."* They are also known by other names such as: *"Sama Dilaut," "Laut,"* or *"Orang Laut"*. Sometimes called *"Sea Gypsies"* these once-boat-dwelling people are traditionally found in the southwestern Philippines (Basilan and Tawi-Tawi areas), northwestern Malaysia and the northern parts of Indonesia down to Johore where legend traces their origin.

There are two tales about the origin of the tribe. The first story involves the Princess Ayesha of Johore and the Sultans of Brunei and Sulu. She preferred the Brunei sultan, but was engaged to the Sulu sultan instead. Escorted by a fleet of war boats, she was sailing towards Sulu when a Brunei fleet, led by their Sultan, intercepted them and took the princess away. The princess' entourage, fearing to go on to Sulu or return to Johore, stayed on the sea, mooring only at uninhabited islands. Some turned to piracy and established pirate dens along North Borneo coasts.

The other Badjao tale says that the ancestors of the Samal ha Laud came from a fishing clan in Johore, Indonesia. A group of boats sailed in search of richer fishing grounds. One night, a typhoon came and they had to anchor by a sandbar. As they were about to rest for the night, their boats suddenly started bucking up and down. They realized they had tied their boats to the nose of a giant manta ray, which had begun to swim round and round in a frantic attempt to unloosen the ropes tied to its nose. The fishers managed to untie their boats, but by then, they had been flung in an island that is unfamiliar to them.

There is also a theory that the Badjaos were originally from the land-based Samal group but branched off into boat dwellers as a result of their occupation. Another theory claims the Badjaos were originally boat dwellers that eventually built stilt houses near fertile fishing grounds.

Regardless of their origin, the Badjao have been driven to near extinction due to the exploitation by the neighboring dominant tribes like the Tausog, the Yakans and even the Christians, disease, starvation and apparent inability to cope with the social changes, they are sometimes referred to also as a *"vanishing tribe."* At present estimates place their number to about a 40,000 in the Philippines.

The Badjaos are peace-loving people, oftentimes to a fault. They would endure all forms of hardship, inconvenience and lost opportunities only to avoid getting into trouble, especially with people not of their own tribe. Hence, they prefer to live in peace by themselves at the coastal fringes of population centers, mangrove areas, coves and islets. With the huge logs which they once used to carve into houseboats becoming scarce (and expensive), their mobile dwellings have since evolved into shanties on stilts – literally a ramshackle ensemble of poles, palm fronds, and if the family is better off, some pieces of miss-cut planks.

Most Badjaos are fishermen (traditionally, all of them were) and they live on the bounties of the sea or on what is left of it. Having lost their traditional fishing grounds due to armed conflict, commercial fishing, pirates and poachers, they are left with meager means of livelihood.

Extreme poverty has forced many of them to resort to begging as a means of survival. Wherever they live, they are considered citizens of the lowest class: ignorant, dirty, stench-smelling and deprived and most people have very low regard for them. In different parts of Mindanao their situation is a picture of complete neglect that has driven whole families to flock to the big cities of Metro Manila, Cebu and Davao to beg in the streets.

The Badjaos are at the receiving end of all the consequences of the systemic on-going insecurities and violence beyond reach of government services.

*A portion of t*he preceding information about the Badjao was taken from a petition letter for the inclusion of the Indigenous People (IP) Samal Bajau Communities in the proposed Bangsamoro Basic Law BBL written and originally published by: Bro. Nicer O. Natulla, JPIC commission Head of the Claretian Missionaries in Maluso, Basilan province Philippines* (January 2015)

Badjao or Goodjao? What Difference Does it Make?

 I have noticed a trend among many individuals and organizations who work among the Badjao to refer to them as "*Goodjao*" and in many cases encourage members of this tribe to call themselves by that name. This is based on a couple of things: a lack of knowledge about the meaning of the name "*Badjao,*" and assuming that the definition of the word "*Bad*" is universal throughout the world. Many may feel that this is a harmless practice, but let me explain why it concerns me.

The word "*Bad*" in the English language is considered to mean something negative and this is also true in many other languages and cultures. However, the word "*Bad*" in some languages can have an entirely different meaning. Here are a few examples of this; in Dutch and Swedish it means "*Bath*", in Gujarati it means "*Following*", in Hindi it means "*After*" and finally in Somali it means "*Sea*" just as it does in the case of our friends the Badjao.

By referring to the Badjao as "*Goodjao*", we are inadvertently causing the people, especially the children, to feel a sense of shame towards their tribes given name and their community whether it be consciously or subconsciously. After all, "*Good*" is the opposite of "*Bad*", just as "*Light*" is to "*Dark*". Would it not be logical then for the Badjao to think that if they are now being called, or being encouraged to call themselves "*Good*", that they must have once been "*Bad*" in the negative sense of the word?

My reason for writing this is to remind those who do trans-cultural work that we must always respect the language and culture of the people we are serving.

In the case of the Badjao, rather than us potentially causing them to have feelings of doubt or uncertainty about themselves by calling them by another name, lets instead encourage them to be proud of not only themselves, but also of their history and their traditions. After all, the Badjao are brave divers, skilled fishermen and extraordinary weavers. They are of royal blood, lords and ladies not of the land, but of the sea.

OUR PROJECTS

BADJAO LEARNING CENTER

Literacy rates among the Badjao in the Philippines are below 10% and fewer than 20% of all Badjao children are enrolled in school. Our learning center targets these marginalized children who otherwise would be found begging in the streets of Davao City.

As funding becomes available, children who attend our learning center are eligible to become a part of the Child Sponsorship Program to attend a local elementary school. Our long-term commitment is to provide access to school for all Badjao children, so that each one may have a chance to realize their educational goals.

CHILD SPONSORSHIP

While our learning center provides children with the basic building blocks of reading, writing and math, this is only a stepping stone which prepares the them for further schooling. We eventually hope to enroll every Badjao child in the Davao region in the public school system.

Most of the children do not have records of birth and an affidavit in lieu of birth certificate is required before enrolling in public school. We assist the children in acquiring the necessary paperwork and assign them a birth date based on interviews with the parents.

Once enrolled in public school the initial amount needed to purchase uniforms, shoes, books, paper, pencils and miscellaneous other school supplies for an elementary student is around $20, and $25 for students entering high school.

When we sponsor students we don't just buy them a uniform, school supplies, and send them on their way; we also provide mentoring, tutoring, and take the time to meet with their teachers throughout the year to monitor their progress.

We also provide funds for transportation, snacks during the student's break time, and purchase materials needed for school projects throughout the year when they are required.

Poverty is much more than it appears on the surface and it has more to do with self worth and value rather than a lack of money and material wealth. Education is the key to alleviating poverty. While everyone who graduates high school and/or continues on to get a degree may not land a high paying job, what they all have gained is a sense of pride. This is the long term benefit of education.

In the short term the child that is in school will no longer be in the streets begging which will greatly lessen the chances of him or her becoming dependent later in life or involved in crime or drugs. There is less chance of them being involved in an accident which may maim or kill them. For young girls being in school lessens the chances of them becoming pregnant at a young age which is a huge contributor to poverty. It also reduces the chances of children becoming victims of abuse and trafficking since a majority of their time will be spent in the classroom rather than on the streets. They will learn better hygiene and health care which will make then healthier and stronger. The benefits go on and on.

Whether or not these children go on to find a high paying job after graduating the benefits of education are still very important. Just having one educated member of a family goes a long way in developing countries like the Philippines.

With an educated member in the household it is less likely that the family will be exploited through unfair contracts and business dealings and they will be less likely to be short changed when transacting with street vendors. The educated family member can teach their parents and siblings the basics as far as reading writing and math and in time the entire family will benefit from a single child in the household going to school.

MICRONUTRIENT DISTRIBUTION

Micronutrient deficiencies in young children can lead to various disorders such as Anemia, Vitamin A Deficiency, and Iodine Deficiency Disorder which lead to impaired motor development and growth, decreased immunity as well as adversely affect intellectual development and mental capacity. For this reason, we have started an in house Micronutrient program at Isla Verde.

We educate the mothers at the Badjao village at Isla Verde about the importance of good nutrition and how to incorporate Micronutrient powders into their children's diet.

One sachet of Micronutrient Powder per child per day provides an adequate intake of vitamins and minerals for children when mixed with food. Each sachet contains a recommended daily allowance of 15 different vitamins and minerals: Vitamins A, D, E, B1, B2, B6, B12, C, Niacin, Folate, Iron, Zinc, Copper, Selenium and Iodine.

Some of the benefits of micronutrients include:

- Improving the body's immune system

- Improving a child's appetite

- Improving a child's ability to learn and develop

- Makes a child clever, strong and active

According to the Philippine Department of Health, micronutrient supplementation has also been shown to reduce:

- The risk from mortality by 23-34%

- Deaths due to measles by about 50%

- Deaths due to diarrhea by about 40%

LIVELIHOOD

With the exception of special occasions such as Christmas or in emergency relief situations, Badjao Outreach has a strict "no handouts" policy. We don't "give fish" as we believe it is actually a stumbling block to sustainable development. However, "Teaching a man to fish" is something we believe in and have embed into all of our programs. We are always working towards an exit strategy so that the Badjao can manage, operate and continue the projects we have developed on their own at some point in the future.

In recent years many of the Badjao families here in Davao have been able to improve their way of living. Rather than begging for alms, a number of them have become entrepreneurs.

Currently "Ukay-Ukay" (The selling of used clothing and shoes) is a profitable business for the Badjao. And while the opportunity is limited, a few of the families have even been able to establish "sari sari stores" (Variety stores) within their community. We have provided several families with the start up capital needed to start their own businesses.

While these businesses are not in line with their traditional ways of livelihood, they are still producing much needed income. The current situation at Isla Verde does not allow for the development of cultural related means of livelihood, but we are hoping to incorporate mat weaving and other more suitable income producing projects in the future.

In the meantime we are experimenting with sewing and creating hand and drawstring bags. This will create income opportunities for those who sew and sell these products.

The Badjao Language

The Language spoken by most Badjao found in the Philippines is Central Sinama. There are thought to be fewer than 150,000 speakers of Central Sinama.

A Few Common Badjao Words and Phrases

Buwatingaru ka? - How are you?
Ahap subu - good morning
Ahap kohap - good afternoon
Ahap sangum - good evening
Sai un nu? - What is your name?
Un ko si Sandara - My name is Sandara.
Pila na umulnu? - How old are you?
Ay hinang nu? - What are you doing?
Ay itu? - What is this?
Ay kinakan nu? - What is your food?
Amangan kita! - Let's eat!
Ahsso aku - I'm full.
Alasig aku - I am happy.
Pila sin itu? - How much is this?
Lisag pila? - What time is it?
Piingga ka? - Where are you going?
Bai ka maingga? - Where have you been?
Palaan na aku - I am leaving.
Piitu ka - Come here.
Pakale ka - listen
Alasa aku ma ka'a. - I love you.

Tabiya - Excuse me
Maingga pat na annu? - Where do you live?
A miningga ka? - Where are you from?
Ai gawinu? - What can I do for you?
Amole na aku - I'm going home.
Amole na kita - Let's go now.
Manjari ka bahā' patta'ku? - May I take your picture?
Mbal tahatiku - I do not understand.
Patibaw sadja aku - I just came to visit.

aho – yes
mbal – no
Onde – baby/child

Manis (Beautiful) Manis kow toongan (You're so beautiful).
Kiit (Few) Kiit du kinakan (The food is few).
Nengko (Sit) Nengko kow ma panengkoan (Sit on the couch).
Nengge (Stand) Nengge kow ma lantey (Stand on the floor).
Ahap sana (Delicious)- Hapsana kinakan milu (The food is delicious there).
Piddi (Aching)- Piddi kok ku (My head is aching).
Palaksu (Jump)- Palaksu kow toongan (You must jump so much).
Nangis (Cry)- Daa kow nangis (Don't cry).

Bagey (Friends) Heka bagey ku. (I have so many friends.)
Kinakan (Food) Ahap sana kinakan naan. (The food is delicious.)
Bilahi (Like) Bilahi aku makau. (I like you.)
Amaleh (Tired) Nimaleh na aku. (I'm so tired)
Danda (Girl) Manis danda eya. (She is beautiful.)
Empon (Teeth) Lanuh toongan empon nu. (Your teeth are so clean.)
Piddi (Painful) Piddi bottong ku. (My stomache is painful.)
Kinaruh (SLEEPY) Si Siva kinaruh sadja. (Siva is always sleepy.)
Sumping (FLOWER) Manis sumping na (The flower is stunning.)
Mangan (Eat) Mangan kow? (Do you wanna eat?)
Ettom (Black) Ettom turung na. (Her veil is black.)
Pahalu (Tomorrow) Pingga kam pahalu? (Where are you going tomorrow?)
Tenaan (Today) Pingga ta bi tenaan? (Where are we going today?)
Pakale (Listen) Pakale kow maaku. (Listen to me.)
Ongka (Sing) Tau aku ngongka. (I know how to sing)

Badjao Girls
By Airyn Sloan

Badjao Girls feet understand
the flows of jeepneys and buses
as they wrestle the wave of
aching hours, rain or shine,
lives in danger; upon counting the days gone by..

To live...

To fit in...

Trying to put a fake smile to the homeland that never been a home...

Why?

As we all see,

Each day they work to the bones,

Collecting paining memories,

Holding their tears upon seeing other children in uniforms
And comfort themselves on flattened cartoon boxes under the bridges,

Along the highways with sacks of cements sewed together

To protect them as roofs and walls

Of what they called Home...

Where hearts' desires slowly dies

Their soring feet rape their fantasies

And to shut their eyes to the rhythmic pain,

The incurable pain,

Pasted on their lives as street children,

Ah! These torturing nights...

The pain I've seen...

When will it end?

We always appreciate the generosity and involvement of people like you, with every contribution going towards providing the Badjao with education, opportunity, and hope.

Donations via Credit/Debit Card, Paypal, or Bank Transfer can be made online by visiting our website at:

Badjao.org/donate

You can also set up monthly recurring donations by visiting the website as well.

Donations in the form of a check or money order can be mailed to the following address:

Badjao Outreach, Inc.
PO Box 222
Eden, NC 27289

Magsukul - Thank you!

After this book was originally published in 2013 a fire destroyed the entire village of the Badjao at Isla Verde, including our learning center. (The fire occurred on April 4, 2014)

Fortunately there were no deaths or serious injuries resulting from the fire, however; following the fire the Badjao were located to a refugee camp and it was there that the problems began. Due to the crowded conditions and poor sanitation there was an outbreak of measles which quickly spread through the camp. There were two dozen deaths that resulted and most of the victims were under three years of age.

As of January 2015, the Badjao have since returned to the site of their original village, but the situation is still far from ideal.

Badjao.org

Made in United States
North Haven, CT
28 July 2024